The Audacity of Prayer is a fresh, uplifting reminder of God's power to work miracles in our lives. Far too often we as believers relegate prayer to the background of our lives, when in reality it is prayer that sustains us and keeps us in awe of God's presence. Through several testimonies of God's miraculous intervention and a detailed investigation of the characteristics of faith, Don Nordin will encourage the reader to live a bold and inspired prayer life. I would highly recommend this book to believers new and old who are in need of a renewed sense of hope and a determination to achieve greater things in the name of the Lord.

—PASTOR MATTHEW BARNETT
COFOUNDER OF THE DREAM CENTER
LOS ANGELES, CALIFORNIA

What you hold in your hands is a powerful new book by my dear friend Pastor Don Nordin. Every time I have ever been around this great man of prayer, authority, and anointing, I have been stirred to go deeper in my relationship with Jesus. In his new book, *The Audacity of Prayer*, you too will experience the transformational hunger for the supernatural things of God. This book is a call back to believe in the miraculous healing power that is part of our inheritance in Christ. As I read this book, I was profoundly moved by the Holy Spirit to expect Him to do the miraculous because "nothing is impossible with God." Each riveting story of God's healing power personally built my faith and inspired me to live a life that goes beyond the norm. This book is a timely message of hope that everyone must read! Thank you, Don, for simply bragging on God. Buckle up—your adventure begins in chapter one!

—PATRICK SCHATZLINE
EVANGELIST, MERCY SEAT MINISTRIES
AUTHOR OF *WHY IS GOD SO MAD AT ME?*

If you would like to experience the supernatural, believe for miracles, and increase your level of expectancy for answers to your prayers, Don Nordin has written a book you must read. *The Audacity of Prayer* clearly outlines principles of prayer that will increase your faith. The documented miracles he shares will give you hope and bolster your enthusiasm. This book will help us all believe that God is just as anxious to demonstrate His healing power in the present and future as He was in the past.

—Dr. Alton Garrison
Assistant general superintendent of
the Assemblies of God
Springfield, Missouri

If you are a believer in the presence of miracles and the power of God at work in our world today, *The Audacity of Prayer* will build your faith chapter by chapter. If you are a skeptic and think there is a clear explanation for everything that does not include God or miraculous intervention, *The Audacity of Prayer* may be the book that begins to change your mind-set. Believer or skeptic, if you find yourself at a place in life that requires a miracle, *The Audacity of Prayer* will drive you to your knees—to pray audacious prayers and receive audacious answers.

—Bishop T. F. Tenney
Focused Light Ministries
Alexandria, Louisiana

Through the absorbing stories of people who have faced incredible odds and the provoking insights on how to overcome every circumstance through a life of prayer, my husband's book *The Audacity of Prayer* will leave you with the revelation that while we can only do what's possible, our God can do the impossible. By the time you finish this book, your faith will be soaring and you will know that God can come through for you in extraordinary ways. A box of tissues is highly recommended for all the rejoicing you will do as you read this power-packed book.

—SUSAN NORDIN
ASSOCIATE PASTOR, CT CHURCH
HOUSTON, TEXAS

The Audacity of Prayer is not your normal, motivational admonition to pray. It provides empirical and theological insight into the value of enhanced relational interaction with the living God. Don Nordin reveals prayer power as a response to God's revelation and our willingness to cultivate personal relationship over religious rituals. God has spoken to us through His Word and Spirit, requiring us and providing us with the privilege to respond intimately and wonderfully with our heart via prayer. This is a must-read for Christians who desire to actually know God and not just know about Him.

—JIM HENNESY
LEAD PASTOR, TRINITY CHURCH
CEDAR HILL, TEXAS

In *The Audacity of Prayer* Don Nordin recounts captivating life stories of real people. He gives compelling examples of documented miracles of divine intervention while making it clear that each individual had to find their own path to experiencing the miraculous. This book will help motivate you to believe for the unbelievable while inspiring you to trust the guidance of the Holy Ghost for your particular situation. Once again we are reminded that when Jesus said, "Ask and ye shall receive," He was talking to you and me!

—ANTHONY MANGUN
LEAD PASTOR, THE PENTECOSTALS OF ALEXANDRIA
ALEXANDRIA, LOUISIANA

Don Nordin's *The Audacity of Prayer* will ignite a passion in your heart to pray and believe God for the miraculous. Pastor Don does not write from the perspective of a theorist. This book is no dry academic treatise. His is a life filled with one miraculous answer to prayer after another. The people of his wonderful CT Church are learning from Pastor Nordin that God is a "right now" God who delights in doing the impossible. I encourage you to read this book with a heart full of expectation. Your miracle is only a prayer away!

—Dr. Scott Camp
International evangelist
Former dean and professor of evangelism,
Southwestern Assemblies of God University

The Audacity of Prayer is a great reminder that prayer is not some mechanical duty that we are obligated to perform—it is a privileged opportunity to develop an intimate relationship with the very One who can answer our prayers! This book is a great reminder that if you believe in Jesus, you can believe in miracles!

—Doug Clay
General treasurer, Assemblies of God
Springfield, Missouri

When it comes to prayer, Don Nordin is a practitioner not a theorist. His book *The Audacity of Prayer* will motivate any reader in his or her prayer life. Don masterfully intertwines solid biblical doctrine regarding prayer, provides detailed accounts of miraculously answered prayer, and shares from his personal walk with God. The result is a dynamic, insightful, and moving work certain to fuel a passion to pray. As I read each retelling of answered prayer, I felt as if I was reading a modern Book of Acts. In page after page I found a new desire to "carry everything to God in prayer." You will be blessed, challenged, and inspired by this book. Don Nordin is a powerful voice for audacious prayer.

—MICHAEL GOLDSMITH
LEAD PASTOR, TIMBER RIDGE CHURCH
CATOOSA, OKLAHOMA

There are many books that are informational and knowledge based. Those of us who love to read understand the importance of those books. Then there are those like *The Audacity of Prayer* that motivate us to believe for the miraculous in our hearts and lives. If you've ever wondered how prayer can change things, you must read *The Audacity of Prayer*. In a day and time when people's faith is being shipwrecked, *The Audacity of Prayer* will anchor your soul in the harbor of the miraculous.

—RANDY VALIMONT
SENIOR PASTOR, GRIFFIN FIRST ASSEMBLY
GRIFFIN, GEORGIA
PRESIDENT OF CALCUTTA MERCY MINISTRIES

Don Nordin has captured the power of "story" in *The Audacity of Prayer*. His unique combination of story and Scripture inspires, challenges, convicts, and motivates us to activate a new level of prayer in our lives—prayer that moves God to move heaven and earth on behalf of His beloved children. This book embodies the passionate, lifelong journey of a man who urgently wants to impart the transformational power of prayer to all who will hear.

—DR. RICK ROSS
LEAD PASTOR, CFA CHURCH
CONCORD, NORTH CAROLINA

Pastor Don Nordin is one of America's great pastors, and he is a powerful preacher of God's Word. But more than anything he is known as a man of prayer. From this position of humility and total dependence upon God, Pastor Nordin has seen hundreds of lives transformed as the miracles of the Book of Acts continue to unfold in the city of Houston, Texas. His "success" in ministry is available to you, for it is simply the power of prayer mixed with faith and the Lord working through and with you!

—ANDY HARRIS
LEAD PASTOR, CENTRAL ASSEMBLY OF GOD
SHREVEPORT, LOUISIANA

THE

AUDACITY

of

Prayer

THE
AUDACITY
of
Prayer

DON NORDIN

CHARISMA
HOUSE

Cover design by Lisa Rae Cox
Design Director: Bill Johnson

Visit the author's website at www.donnordinministries.com.

Library of Congress Cataloging-in-Publication Data:
Nordin, Don.
  The audacity of prayer : when ordinary people receive healing answers from god / Don Nordin.
        pages cm
  Summary: "God is still in the business of performing miracles. He desires to produce one in your life right now! The word audacity declares that one has stepped from the ranks of convention and normal expectation into daring, uncharted territory. This is especially so with regard to our prayers. Jesus Himself calls us to a life of daring prayer. The Audacity of Prayer shares the stories of modern-day miracles that have occurred as a result of audacious prayer including when:
  ISBN 978-1-62136-257-9 (paperback) -- ISBN 978-1-62136-258-6 (e-book)
  1. Prayer--Christianity. I. Title.
  BV220.N67 2014
  248.3'2--dc23
                              2013039543

While the author has made every effort to provide accurate telephone numbers and Internet addresses at the time of publication, neither the publisher nor the author assumes any responsibility for errors or for changes that occur after publication.

AUTHOR'S NOTE: Some names, places, and identifying details with regard to stories in this book have been changed to help protect the privacy of the individuals involved. All testimonies have been published with written permission from the subjects of the stories.

First edition

14 15 16 17 18 — 9 8 7 6 5 4 3 2 1
Printed in the United States of America

To my parents, who taught me to believe God for the miraculous...

CONTENTS

ACKNOWLEDGMENTS

*T*HERE IS ONE name featured on the cover of this book, but there are many people who helped make this work possible. I owe them all a sincere debt of gratitude.

First, to Susan Nordin, my faithful wife and ministry partner of more than thirty-five years—thank you for your support and encouragement. You remained by my side through some very difficult days of apparent defeat as well as some exhilarating days of tremendous victory. No matter what we faced, you were always a consummate encourager, urging me to do all that God had placed in my heart to do. I am so grateful that God brought you into my life.

I would also like to thank my two children, Jason and Larissa, as well as my son-in-law, Jeremy, and my daughter-in-law, Kim. Thank you for believing in me and for blessing me with my precious grandchildren, Braden and Rylee. They have certainly been the icing on the cake of life!

Steve Lestarjette, thank you for being such a tremendous friend and encourager for the last ten-plus years. You helped me get my first book, *Working at God's Altar*, published, and during that process you helped me to develop a passion for writing. Thank you for assisting me again with *The Audacity of Prayer*. You spent many hours poring over the manuscript and recommending changes, and all your hard work shows. Thank you, friend.

Ellyn McDonald, you work a full-time job but you still manage to proofread all my sermon manuscripts and other projects I send your way, sometimes on the spur of the moment. Thank you for again working your magic on each chapter of this book.

Evangelist Pat Schatzline, thank you for introducing me to the Charisma Media family. Without this introduction, bringing *The Audacity of Prayer* to publication would have been much more difficult. And to the team at Charisma Media, you have been absolutely wonderful. A special thanks goes to my editor, Adrienne Gaines, who has been a tremendous resource throughout this process. I appreciate so much the advice and direction you have given along the way.

Last but not least I am grateful to the board, staff, and leadership team of CT Church in Houston, Texas. You were so patient with me as I wrote and traveled to various preaching appointments. As a result of my extensive travels, you've had to bear a much greater load of responsibility. Yet everyone in this great church operates from the philosophy that my writing and travels are an extension of the footprint of the ministry of CT Church. So rather than complain about my absence, you prayed for my effectiveness in ministry. Truly, I am blessed to pastor the greatest church on earth.

And to you, the reader, it is my sincere prayer that *The Audacity of Prayer* will be more than an enjoyable read. I pray that it will jump-start your faith to believe God for miracles in your life and circle of influence.

DOING HIS WORK FIRST,
—DON NORDIN

PREFACE

*Y*OU DO NOT have because you do not ask" (James 4:2). If we truly believe the Bible means what it says, *what then* might we have received had we asked? What victory? What healing or provision? What protection, restoration, or redemption? What glory and worship might our heavenly Father have received if we had but asked His help in our time of trouble?

Why then do we not ask? What prevents us? Is the way blocked to God? Do we suppose Him limited or uncaring?

Quickly we find the open door: "Come boldly to the throne of grace," the writer of Hebrews exhorts us, "that we may obtain mercy and find grace to help in time of need" (Heb. 4:16). "Eye has not seen, nor ear heard, nor have entered into the heart of man the things which God *has prepared* for those who love Him" (1 Cor. 2:9, emphasis added).

The preparation is done, our answer is waiting, if only we come boldly and ask! We have no other precondition or criteria to achieve the answer God has made ready for us except one: we must believe! "Whatever things you ask when you pray, believe that you receive them, and you will have them" (Mark 11:24). "Let him ask in faith, with no doubting" (James 1:6).

Notice the vast extent of His invitation: "*Whatever* things you ask!" What is overlooked in that majestic word? Is any need? Any concern or fear? Any pain or hopeless circumstance?

The One who answers is ready. The provision has been prepared. His abilities and compassions are limitless. Yet we often do not ask, we do not contend for our miracle, and His wonderful, sufficient response remains in the storehouse of His blessing.

Is it possible that God uses our adversities to teach us the benefit of asking? Does He let distress and dilemma have their way for a season while He waits to hear our cry? Does He use our desperate need to turn our eyes upward where we will find our Father listening and our answer at the ready?

ASK, AND YOU WILL RECEIVE!

I know God is willing to move heaven and earth on our behalf. I saw it first as a small boy, as God healed a father who had been crushed beneath a two-ton tree. I've seen that power repeatedly as a pastor and intercessor, watching in silent amazement as God has raised the crippled, spared unborn children from certain death, restored financial fortunes, secured redemption, and healed countless dozens whose cause was written off as lost.

Some of these stories are in the pages that follow. They have been told by ordinary people with extraordinary needs who cried out in desperation and found God attentive and moving to the scene even before they spoke. The only common denominator linking these amazing stories is this: each had the audacity to ask the ridiculous, the impossible. Their testimony is consistent: "I sought the LORD, and He heard me, and delivered me from all my fears" (Ps. 34:4).

Let these stories serve as your encouragement and example. Let loose your caution. Throw off your doubts. Look up. Cry out to your loving Father above—and receive.

One

WHY PRAY?

*I*N TODAY'S CULTURE prayer has been all but forgotten. Like a powerful muscle that atrophies from neglect, the believer who fails to pray becomes extremely carnal and rife with all kinds of issues. A believer who neglects prayer is like a fish that avoids water. Prayer is literally the lifeline of the Christian.

The word *prayer* has become cliché in this culture. It has become a term to use when we want to provide encouragement but have nothing of substance to offer. Believers and non-believers alike use it freely saying, "I'll keep you in my prayers," then never actually pray at all. The promise to pray serves as little more than a dismissive end to an uncomfortable conversation to which there are no apparent answers.

When a national tragedy strikes, even those who have had a hand in kicking God out of the schools—the government, the courts, and the public arena—suddenly start talking about prayer. The truth is, God and prayer cannot be expelled from any of these arenas as long as believers continue to walk the earth. Prayer will never be removed from schools as long as Christians are required to take tests!

For a Christian, prayer is the same as breathing is to the natural body. Prayer is absolutely the survival mechanism for Christ followers.

As a pastor I have told people I would be praying for them, and though I diligently followed through to do so, I left the conversation thinking, "I wish I could do something more." Like others, I sometimes feel praying is the least I can do, when, in fact, it is the greatest and most productive thing we can do for those who are facing the battering ram of life. Life has a way of extracting hope from its participants, but prayer reestablishes hope. Hope anchors the soul and allows the fresh sunshine of the love of God to come pouring in. Like the breaking of the day after a dark night of despair, prayer causes the believer to emerge from trouble with a new lease on life and anticipation for the future.

In his booklet *Master Secrets of Prayer* Cameron Thompson writes: "There comes a time, in spite of our soft, modern ways, when we must be desperate in prayer, when we must wrestle, when we must be outspoken, shameless and importunate."[1] This statement sums up perfectly what I mean when I talk about audacious prayer. Prayer can take the impossible and turn it into new opportunities for the future.

Before meeting his brother, Esau, Jacob prayed all night. He was determined to receive assurance from the Lord that his brother would not kill him the next day. So intense was that prayer meeting that Jacob emerged with a name change and a limp that would mark his every step for the rest of his life.

Have you ever had the audacity to go before the Lord with such passion for the burden you were carrying that you decided you would not leave until you were able to emerge with an answer? The desperate cry of the righteous in a prayer closet strikes a chord in the heart of God!

The Bible is a book about fervent prayer and the resulting answers to those prayers. From Genesis to Revelation the power of audacious prayer is emphasized virtually from chapter to chapter and verse to verse. One would be hard pressed to read the Bible without coming to the conclusion that prayer actually does change things. In fact, prayer changes everything. Faith and prayer are the tandem vehicles that move things from the realm of the spirit to the natural arena. They cause the unseen to become reality.

Contemporary Christians will do well to once again pray over their families and lives in an audacious manner. The promise to reverse negative circumstances is only guaranteed to those who pray. "If My people who are called by My name will humble themselves, and pray and seek My face, and turn from their wicked ways, then I will hear from heaven, and will forgive their sin and heal their land" (2 Chron. 7:14). If we humble ourselves in prayer and turn from our wicked ways, He will "heal our land." What does He mean by "our land"? Our land is not only our nation and world but also our lives. He has promised to heal the lives of those who are serious about prayer and righteous living.

Jesus Himself implored us to pray audaciously. "Then He spoke a parable to them, that men always ought to pray and not lose heart" (Luke 18:1). "Ask, and it will be given to you; seek, and you will find; knock, and it will be opened to you. For everyone who asks receives, and he who seeks finds, and to him who knocks it will be opened" (Matt. 7:7–8). These are not the words of some popular success guru; these are the words of Jesus! What is promised to those who pray and don't lose heart?

- Ask and you will receive
- Seek and you will find what you are searching for
- Knock and doors will be opened to you

The words of Jesus provide a wonderful assurance to those who will take the time to be diligent in prayer. Prayer transcends all religions. Every religion has its own idea of the proper means, times, and reasons for prayer. Various religions pray to a diversity of gods:

- Islamic believers pray to Allah five times a day.

- Buddhist believers pray to Buddha.

- Hindu believers pray to hundreds of gods twice a day.

- Jewish believers pray to Yahweh three times a day.

- Catholics pray to Mary.

- All Christians pray to Jehovah.

What sets apart the prayers of Christians from all others is that, while other religions pray to dead deities, Christians pray to the God who is very much alive.

Peter Kreeft, author and professor of theology at Boston College, made this observation concerning prayer: "I strongly suspect that if we saw all the difference even the tiniest of our prayers to God make, and all the people those little prayers were destined to affect, and all the consequences of those prayers down through the centuries, we would be so paralyzed with awe at the power of prayer that we would be unable to get up off of our knees for the rest of our lives."[2] What a great admonition concerning prayer! Only eternity will reveal the effects prayer has had on this world and in the lives of untold scores of individuals through the centuries.

We often make the mistake of believing that prayer is only about getting stuff from God. While it is true that prayer is the delivery route for things in the life of the believer, it is much more than that. Prayer develops trust in the heart of the believer that God absolutely will perform what He has said. For the believer, all intimacy with God is born out of trust that has been developed in times of prayer. Intimacy leads to faith and audacious praying. Faith and audacious prayer produce the miraculous.

Individuals who have a consistent prayer life over the long haul can testify to personally witnessing the power of the living Christ at work in their lives. They trust God and they trust His Word. In doing so, these Christ followers become examples of how life is to be lived.

Praying people become persons of great faith. Thomas Watson, the Puritan writer, said, "Faith is to prayer what the feather is to the arrow. Faith feathers the arrow of prayer, and makes it fly swifter, and pierce the throne of grace."[3] For the believer, prayer is the aiming device for our journey. I can personally testify to the fact that numerous times as I have met with God before beginning my day, He warned me of impending danger and directed me around pitfalls that I did not even know existed.

Many times I have gone into my daily prayer time on the verge of making a very important decision, and during my time with Him I was made to know that what I was about to do would be a mistake. He gave me new direction and allowed me to navigate through issues that involved a lot of individuals. When that has occurred, 100 percent of the time the new direction was absolutely the right decision. The life of a Christian who does not pray is like an arrow that has no specific target! A prayerless life is dangerous to everyone in its circle of influence.

In the first-century-church miracles were in abundance. When one looks at the behavior of these believers, we readily discover that prayer was one of the foundational stones of their existence. I believe God is calling His children back to their prayer closets. If we will begin to commune with Him and possess the audacity to pray, the miraculous will once again become the norm.

Desperation is the environment that miracles are birthed in. Most people never contend for a miracle until the possibility of all human help has been exhausted. That is not intended to be an indictment; it is just a fact that we try everything in our power to alleviate the dilemma that we face. Then, when we have come to the end of ourselves, we turn to God in audacious prayer. That is just the way we are wired. God knows this, and He is always standing at the end of the path with His hands outstretched saying, "Come unto Me, all you who labor and are heavy laden, and I will give you rest" (Matt. 11:28).

Speaking of the miracle of the Red Sea crossing, Matthew Henry said, "Their fear set them a praying, and that was a good effect of it. God brings us into straits, that He may bring us to our knees."[4] Some would question: If God wanted the Israelites out of Egypt and out of the hands of Pharaoh, why did He not open the Red Sea before they arrived? I think there are several reasons:

- He wanted them to see what He could do in response to the people and their leaders crying out to Him.

- He wanted to even the score with those who had abused and mistreated His people.

- He wanted to deliver the weapons of the Egyptians into the hands of the Israelites because they were going to need them for future battles.

- He wanted to raise the level of their faith to endure the challenges of the wilderness and Canaan.

Prayer worked at the Red Sea, and it works now!

VITAL REASONS FOR PRAYER

The Word of God makes it clear: prayer is the act of communicating with God. If prayer is the means of communication between an earthly believer and his heavenly Father, the earthly believer should look forward to this means of speaking with his Father and mentor! Let's explore seven vital reasons for prayer.

1. Prayer is required to be forgiven.

"Blessed is he whose transgression is forgiven, whose sin is covered. Blessed is the man to whom the LORD does not impute iniquity, and in whose spirit there is no deceit. When I kept silent, my bones grew old through my groaning all the day long. For day and night Your hand was heavy upon me; my vitality was turned into the drought of summer. I acknowledged my sin to You, and my iniquity I have not hidden. I said, 'I will confess my transgressions to the LORD,' and You forgave the iniquity of my sin. For this cause everyone who is godly shall pray to You in a time when You may be found; surely in a flood of great waters they shall not come near him" (Ps. 32:1–6). *The Audacity of Prayer* is a book about miracles, but the greatest miracle that could ever be performed is for God to forgive sin. The process of forgiveness looks like this:

- *Acknowledgment.* Forgiveness of sins begins with an individual verbalizing through prayer his sinful condition: "I acknowledged my sin to You" (v. 5).

- *Confession.* "I will confess my transgressions to the LORD" (v. 5).

- *Forgiveness.* "You forgave the iniquity of my sin" (v. 5).

One cannot be forgiven by thinking he is sorry for his sin. One cannot be forgiven by having good intentions. The only way a person can be forgiven is by confessing sin before a holy God. Prayer is the initial act of a believer's journey with God, and prayer is the impetus of that journey from spiritual birth to the grave.

2. Prayer is required to develop an intimate relationship with God.

"I love the Lord because he hears my prayers and answers them. Because he bends down and listens, I will pray as long as I breathe!

Death stared me in the face—I was frightened and sad. Then I cried, 'Lord, save me!' How kind he is! How good he is! So merciful, this God of ours! The Lord protects the simple and the childlike; I was facing death, and then he saved me. Now I can relax. For the Lord has done this wonderful miracle for me. He has saved me from death, my eyes from tears, my feet from stumbling. I shall live! Yes, in his presence—here on earth!" (Ps. 116:1–9, TLB).

The writer here lets us know he is a praying person and the habit of prayer has caused him to know that God hears and answers prayer. In fact, as one reads through these verses, the intimacy between the writer and his God is striking. The practice of prayer led to an intimate relationship between God and the psalmist: "He answers my prayers." "He bends down and listens." "I will pray as long as I breathe." "How kind he is." "How good he is." "So merciful, this God of ours." "He saved me."

As I mentioned earlier, for the believer all intimacy is born out of trust. Through his prayer life the psalmist learned to trust God. We should practice prayer for the purpose of developing intimacy with God. No prayer, no intimacy.

3. Prayer is required to maintain purity.

A believer can break fellowship with God while serving in various roles. Serving does not promote purity, nor does it insulate one from failing. The only thing that can prevent one from being caught up in a sinful lifestyle is a consistent, audacious prayer life. Believers who have a daily prayer time that they are faithful to are much less likely to backslide. When we are tempted to sin, the fact that we know we are meeting with God later in the day or the next morning can keep us from committing sin. A believer who is consistent in prayer knows that sin causes him to dread his prayer time. A consistent prayer life causes one to quit sinning, or sin will cause the believer to quit praying. The choice is left to the believer.

I choose to keep praying and quit sinning rather than keep sinning and quit praying.

Daily prayer produces purity in our lives. Holiness is still the order of the day! Consider the words of Jesus: "Blessed are the pure in heart, for they shall see God" (Matt. 5:8).

There is no doubt we live in a very wicked culture. As a result we are constantly confronted with the temptation of doing things the world's way when really we need to act and react like our Father in heaven. In our journey the only way we can hope to live according to God's standards is to have a consistent prayer life that develops purity within and manifests itself in every action we take.

4. Prayer is required to walk in faith.

Faith is a very important component in the life of a believer. "But without faith it is impossible to please him: for he that cometh to God must believe that he is, and that he is a rewarder of them that diligently seek him" (Heb. 11:6, KJV).

Prayer is essential in the development of faith. "So Jesus answered and said to them, 'Assuredly, I say to you, if you have faith and do not doubt, you will not only do what was done to the fig tree, but also if you say to this mountain, "Be removed and be cast into the sea," it will be done. And whatever things you ask in prayer, believing, you will receive'" (Matt. 21:21–22). In thirty-nine years of ministry I have yet to meet one person I believed to have great faith who did not have a consistent prayer life.

According to Romans 12:3, every believer begins his spiritual journey with exactly the same amount of faith. "God hath dealt to every man *the* measure of faith" (KJV, emphasis added). When I read this verse, I often picture the Father holding a specific unit of measure and doling out faith to each of us. The level of faith a believer is capable of attaining depends on how one goes about exercising his faith. The exercising of faith is directly tied to our prayer life! We should pray, making our requests known to God. When He answers our prayer, our faith rises to a new level. Each prayer we see answered enables us to believe God for larger things. As we walk this process out, we are pleasing God. We must develop a prayer life to intentionally grow our faith!

"All things are possible to him that believeth" (Mark 9:23, KJV). Please make a mental note that "all things" do not necessarily come to those who ask; they come to those who believe! Consistent prayer grows our faith, and our faith unlocks the door to the storehouse of God. The expansion of our faith does not come easily:

- Our faith will be tried.

- We must discipline our minds to act on faith.

- Patience must be exercised to walk the faith life.

- Only the courageous exercise God-honoring faith.

What is the end of faith? The victory of faith! Faith brings about a good result.

5. Prayer is required to walk in freedom.

Take a look around you; people are grappling with addictions and phobias of all kinds. Sadly, the bondage of believers often mirrors that of the world. These things can be broken through the power of prayer. Psalm 34 lays out the freedom God affords through prayer. In this passage we are told that the Lord will do the following things in response to the prayer of the believer:

- Deliver us from fear (v. 4)

- Save us from our trouble (v. 6)

- Guard and deliver us (v. 7)

- Be good to those who trust in Him (v. 8)

- Supply all needs (v. 9)

- Hear us when we pray (v. 15)

- Redeem us (v. 22)

We are to receive these things through:

- Crying out to Him (vv. 6, 17)

- Trusting Him (v. 8)

- Fearing Him (vv. 7, 9)

- Refraining from lying (v. 13)

- Humbling ourselves (v. 18)

- Serving Him (v. 22)

God promises great blessings to His people, but many of these blessings require our active participation. In this instance our participation is a consistent prayer life. Prayer is a requirement of living an overcoming Christian life. If we hope to live free, we must be people of prayer.

6. Prayer is required to persevere.

My definition of persistence is the steadfast determination to complete a task without regard to the sacrifice that it will require. By its nature the Christian life demands a boatload of persistence. Any achievement worthy of the effort it requires merits the investment of persistence.

I believe two things are required for a Christian to make the commitment necessary to persist in achieving the will of God:

- *Become a person of prayer.* It is a fact that praying
  people are persistent people. Prayerlessness produces

a lack of persistence. The reason? Persistence is born out of intimacy, and intimacy with God is not possible without a prayer life.

- *Know whom we serve and whose vision we are striving for.* If we are sure it is His purpose we are serving and His goals we are striving to achieve, we become very confident that He will bring it to pass. No matter what long shot His will appears to be in one's life, if we are people of prayer and know we are going for His will, we can patiently endure the days when there seems to be no movement in the circumstances. We know He will bring it to pass.

Winston Churchill is quoted as saying, "The nose of the Bulldog has been slanted backwards so that he can breathe while holding on!"[5] We must become people who have hearts that will not be dissuaded from doing the will of God. We must develop bulldog tenacity in pursuing the purposes of God! We should be people of prayer because it will cause us to be steady and persistent.

7. Prayer is required to have power with God.

Most people would like to have power with God, so why don't we? There are no shortcuts to God's power supply. The path to God's power source leads through His prayer room! The bottom line is this: no prayer, no power. This probably answers the questions heard echoing through churches all across America: "Where are the miracles?" "What must we do to see His miracles?" "Where is His power?"

Jesus spoke of His desire for believers to continue the string of miracles He had begun. "And these signs will follow those who believe: In My name they will cast out demons; they will speak with new tongues; they will take up serpents; and if they drink anything deadly, it will by no means hurt them; they will lay hands on the sick, and they will recover" (Mark 16:17–18).

Why do you suppose God set the distribution of miracles up in a way that they flow through those who pray?

- Praying people are intimately connected to God to the point of developing a heart like Him.

- Praying people see things as God sees them.

- Praying people hear things as God hears them.

- Praying people are humble, not allowing pride to enter when a miracle occurs.

The prayers of righteous people are a source of great power to the world. We should pray so we will be capable of allowing God to dispense miracles through us to a world that desperately needs them!

Will you commit yourself to begin each day with fifteen minutes of prayer? If one is to be successful in living in a way that pleases the Lord, prayer is essential!

In this book you are going to read stories of modern-day miracles that have occurred as a result of audacious prayer. God reacts to our bold, desperate, audacious prayers! It is my hope that as you read these accounts of modern-day miracles, your prayer life will be enhanced and your faith will begin to soar once again.

Friend, be encouraged. God is still in the business of performing miracles. He desires to produce one in your life right now!

Two

CAN YOU GIVE THANKS?

*L*IFE SEEMS TO have a way of throwing curveballs when we are least expecting them and at times when we are ill-prepared to deal with them. All of us have experienced times when our plans were set, we were planning our work and working our plan, and then out of nowhere something develops that turns everything upside down. As Christians we must always remember that God works all things for our good (Rom. 8:28). That is not to say that all things *are* good—only that if we exercise patience, keep a good attitude, and do not lose faith, God will find a way to turn all things for our good.

Another thing to remember in difficult times is that we are to keep ourselves in a continual state of thankfulness. "Rejoice always, pray without ceasing, in everything give thanks; for this is the will of God in Christ Jesus for you" (1 Thess. 5:16–18). I would certainly admit that living the thankful life is a pretty tough assignment during difficult seasons. We must remember that the Word of God never calls upon us to do things we are not capable of doing! Then it stands to reason that if we have been commanded to "rejoice always" and to "give thanks in all things," it is within our reach to do so, no matter what is going on around us.

The beneficial thing about being tested is that we eventually have a testimony that can be shared and used for the good of others. I dare say that most people prefer an untested life, but the truth is, we will all be tested and sometimes to the very limit. Once we have been tested, we emerge as a vessel fit for service. In the case of my dad and mom, Euel and Esther Nordin, the aforementioned verses had to be practiced through a season that lasted for almost five years.

To my parents, my older sister, and myself the memories of a fateful day in July of 1963 are as vivid today as when they happened fifty years ago. My father had been raised in central Arkansas and because of difficult economic times had dropped out of school in the eighth grade to go to work in a sawmill to help make a living for his family. Born the fifth of eight children, he had to pull his weight, just as all the others who were old enough to work. It was a matter of survival.

Dad later attended a Bible college and then a trade school. As many young people of his generation did, Dad eventually migrated to California in search of work and a better life. While in California he met and married the love of his life, my mom, Esther Wallace Nordin. They were married on his twenty-first birthday. I guess you could say he never got to be his own boss! Soon after marriage Uncle Sam enlisted my dad into military service and shipped him off to Germany, far, far away from his bride.

After returning home from military service, Euel became the father of three children, two girls and one boy. For several years he worked in the timber industry in northern California, working in sawmills as well as cutting timber. Eventually we moved to Phillipsville, near Eureka, California. Phillipsville had a familiar feeling to it. It was much like the town of Laytonville, where my parents met. It was there in Laytonville that my dad first began to feel a call from God to become a pastor. He sensed the Lord directing him to lead a small nearby church, but he didn't feel qualified or ready.

16

"No, Lord," he said. "I can't do that." And that was the end of it, he thought.

Though he did not begin his pastoral ministry, he did begin to "fill in" at numerous small churches in the mountains of northern California. He never turned down an opportunity to preach whenever asked, but pastoring was another thing. He knew that dealing with people day in and day out could be demanding, and finances would always be in short supply. Dad had a young family of five to feed, and what he needed was work, a real job with a real paycheck. He needed to make "good money" so he could provide for his family.

At age thirty-one Dad was working with his brother-in-law, cutting timber for a lumber company in the mountains northeast of Myers Flat. The five of us were living in an eight-foot-wide mobile home my parents had recently purchased, and Dad had a good job. Mom and Dad were very happy and blessed to have each other and a few humble comforts. They knew they were not rich and were probably not on a track to become rich, but they understood the things a person can acquire should not define their success in life.

My dad's work was physically taxing and very dangerous. He had to get up at two in the morning to prepare for work and then ride with my uncle in his old Jeep up to the logging camp north of Myers Flat. Even though I wasn't quite four years old, I remember waiting at the end of the road late in the afternoon listening intently for my uncle's Jeep so I could see my dad and ride on the running board back to our mobile home.

"It was hard work," Dad remembers. "We had to get up so early and drive those winding roads in the dark. Then we would be on our feet all day, wearing heavy boots and carrying all our equipment."

Each morning the crew was given a map of the area where they were to cut logs, and then each of them would go his way to fulfill his assignments. The workers were given specific areas and told to cut all marketable timber as they went and to keep a safe distance from other loggers. It was exhausting work, which they carried out in all types of weather. An added challenge was that the work was being done at high altitude. The thin air made breathing difficult.

At five-foot-nine and one hundred forty pounds, Dad was lean and strong. He enjoyed working with his hands and was very good at his job. He remembers, "I never got tired of the smell of clean air and timber." The workday of a logger began at first light and lasted until about three in the afternoon; he then went home to his family while there was still daylight.

Logging is a dangerous trade; there are no safe jobs in the entire industry. Dad explains: "You had to be very careful. Trees grew close together. You might cut one and watch it fall into another tree. When the branches at the top of the tree get into a bind and cannot move, the trunk may lash about in any direction. So when we cut a tree, we made sure we stepped away as quickly as possible. It was never routine; you were never quite sure what might happen as the tree was falling."

On July 23, a clear but hot summer day in the mountains, the unexpected happened. The day had unfolded as it normally did: Dad was on the road up the mountain before daylight and trudged through the brush in heavy boots with chain saw and gas can to fell fifty-foot firs on a gentle slope. Around three in the afternoon, just before quitting time, Dad says, "I saw two nice trees growing close together and told myself those would be the last ones of the day. I was going to fell those two and call it a day because I was really tired. Working all day in a patch of thick underbrush and carrying a chain saw in those conditions drain your energy."

The tree he chose to cut first was rather ordinary for the area. "It wasn't particularly large like some California firs," he recounts. "I suspect it was sixty feet tall and twenty-four inches through the center." The challenges of the day had made him weary and sluggish. "I wasn't moving as fast as I normally did," he says. "I was just tired, that's all."

Perhaps that explains why he was not able to step away quickly enough as the tree began to fall. He watched in horror, his chain saw still revving, as the top of the tree he had cut crashed into the second tree he had planned to fell next. He saw the branches catch, putting the falling tree suddenly in a bind. Trying to respond to gravity, the trunk of the falling tree jumped from the stump and came crashing down upon my dad. It moved faster than a bullet; its weight punched like a powerful fist downward into his midsection below his rib cage. Its sheer force took him off his feet and drove him like a hammer against a stake into the ground. "I didn't see it coming," he explains.

Slammed hard into solid dirt by the weight of the tree, he was unable to move, but miraculously he never lost consciousness. He was still alive and could think. More importantly, he could pray.

THE SUPERNATURAL HAND OF GOD

Praying was as natural to my dad as breathing. In fact, he was almost always praying. The most vivid memories of my childhood were of my dad praying. Whether he was driving the highways or cutting trees, his mind was rarely settled on anything other than the goodness of God. Perhaps he wasn't talking or singing aloud, but one could be certain that Dad was always "on the line" to God.

So what he did next was instinctive. It came from a person in desperate trouble who happened to walk through every day aware of the presence of a powerful, unseen friend. Smashed into the ground like a sack of crushed ice, he cried out to God.

He says, "So much goes through your mind in a split second. I saw my whole family pass before my eyes. I saw my wife and my little children, and I knew they needed me. At the same time I knew I was dying; I could feel my breath leaving, so I gathered my strength and whispered, 'Oh Lord, don't let me die.'"

What seemed like hours could not have been more than a second or two, as the falling tree was still in motion. The flailing tree trunk that had chopped into my dad's midsection and hammered him into the ground immediately bounced up and made ready to crash upon him one final time. He was watching this scene play out like a bad movie in slow motion, but his body was broken and unable to move. He was as limp as a rag doll, left vulnerable and powerless against whatever came next.

Then, with the trunk of the sixty-foot fir driving down toward him one more time, another miracle happened. "Something moved me," he says now, through tears. "It was supernatural. I was not able to move at all, but when the trunk of that tree crushed me and for a split second bounced into the air, I felt a hand drag me in an instant out from beneath the path of the tree. I wasn't pulled sideways; I was snatched headfirst out of the path of the descending tree."

This all happened in a blur; an unseen, inexplicable hand moved him headfirst in one motion more than six feet, until his entire body was miraculously removed from the path of the descending tree.

"I knew it was God," he says. "And that told me so much. One second I knew I was dying; I felt my breath leaving me. The next I knew God wanted me to live! I knew I was going to survive, no matter what."

The hand that moved Dad to safety put him exactly where he would escape the rage of the falling tree. He lay on his back, his chain saw beside him, and began calling out with what strength he had remaining, hoping to catch the attention of his brother-in-law, who was still cutting timber.

"He couldn't hear me, of course. He was on the other side of the slope. I could hear his chain saw and realized he couldn't hear me over the noise. So I lay there until I heard his saw get quiet, then called again."

Surprisingly he finally did hear Dad and came running. When he saw Dad, he immediately went to get help. "There was no blood; that was the amazing thing," Dad remembers. "I wasn't cut. But the tree had shot through my midsection. I knew something was wrong with my stomach and intestines. I knew my sternum was way out of place. I thought my hip might be broken. I can't describe the pain. It was horrible."

My uncle picked up my dad, put him on his back, and headed for the landing where the fallen, harvested trees were piled. After carrying Dad for a considerable distance, he met other loggers who were carrying a stretcher. They placed Dad on it and carried him to the nearest vehicle.

Dad says, "I never knew there was a stretcher in the woods. To this day I don't know where it came from."

Riding on the back of an old Jeep pickup, Dad was taken to the hospital in nearby Garberville. "Those were unfinished mountain roads we went over," he says. "They were hardly roads at all; more like rutted trails through the underbrush. Every turn and bounce of that Jeep made the pain shoot through me until I thought I would pass out. All I could do was pray and try to get through it."

The hospital at Garberville had three doctors on staff. The one needed most, a surgeon, had left that day for a week of vacation. "They didn't know what to do with me," Dad says. "I was so badly crushed that they could not do the most basic thing, which was to move me. There was no way of knowing what my internal injuries were without surgery, but the surgeon was out of town and would not be back for a week."

When the medical staff needed to move him, they attempted to do so using a sheet, but even that caused unbearable pain. They basically left him lying there for a week with no real attempt to discover what his injuries were. The focus of the first week was pain management, and that was administered with very high doses of morphine.

My mother was called when my dad first arrived at the hospital. Upon receiving the news of the accident, Mom quickly gathered up her three children—Linda, who was six; Zoe, who was six months; and me, almost four years old at the time, and we made a mad dash for Garberville. My mom remembers battling through tears as she drove through the very treacherous mountain roads to the hospital.

She says in the backseat I found an altar on the floorboard, where I prayed for my dad during that whole trip to the hospital. "I've always believed there was something about those prayers that made a difference," Dad says. "You don't have to teach a child to pray. If you teach him to love God, he will know what to do."

I know it is difficult to believe that a fifty-three-year-old man can remember the details of an incident that occurred when he was barely four. Nonetheless, I remember that day in vivid detail. When my mother received the news of the accident, I could see the panic on her face. All I could do was say over and over, "Please, God, don't let my daddy die." My parents were then, and continue to be today, my heroes.

The trip to the hospital was in the family car, a 1963 Chevrolet Super Sport two-door hardtop. That particular model had a hump in the back floorboard where the drive train and transmission were. I recall straddling that hump with my face buried in the backseat, praying over and over, "God, please don't let my daddy die." I now believe that the Lord took a terrible accident and used it to create faith in small boy. From that incident to the writing of this book about miracles, fifty years later, I have never doubted that God is willing and able to do miracles in the lives of His people.

All We Could Do Was Pray

The next week can only be described as a long critical wait for everyone involved. Dad explains, "There was nothing they could do, and all I knew to do was pray. Despite the heavy doses of morphine, the pain was unbearable."

There were X-rays—"too many to count"—and every movement caused excruciating pain. He was taken from the emergency room and settled into a room with another patient, an elderly man whose name he does not recall.

"Every now and then my hip would hurt so bad I would scream. I never realized how much I was screaming or how loud, but it must have been quite a lot because the other patient kept asking for sleeping pills."

Everyone expected Dad to die. "The man next to me said as much. I met him sometime later, and he asked me how in the world I survived all that. 'None of us expected you to live,' the man told me."

Waiting a week for surgery while suffering unknown but extensive internal injuries took a heavy toll. "I grew worse every day," Dad confesses. "I could sense I was going downhill. Even so, I never allowed myself to believe I was going to die. I kept praying, remembering that God had pulled me headfirst to safety when it counted most. I knew He had a purpose for my life, and I believed that if He went to the trouble of pulling me from beneath the tree, He would not let me die.

"The Lord and I did some serious talking that week," he recalls. "I told Him, 'Lord, if You will get me out of here, I will go where You want me to go and do what You want me to do.' I made up my mind I would never say no to the Lord again. Finally, seven days after the accident, the surgeon returned from vacation. I could tell by the look on his face that I was in a very critical condition."

Dad remembers that when the doctor took one look at him, he stated with a real sense of urgency, "We have to do surgery tonight; this can't wait." Just prior to that emergency exploratory surgery, a local pastor making rounds at the hospital stepped inside the hospital room. My dad remembers, "I had never met him before, but he took an interest in me. He prayed over me before I was taken to the operating room. I appreciated that."

The next day, after reviving from the effects of anesthesia, Dad recalls, "The pastor returned bearing news. Leaning over the bed, he said, 'Man, you are a miracle. You had gangrene in your stomach; the doctor had to clean out the gangrene before he could repair things.'"

Anyone who knows anything about medicine would readily agree that an untreated internal injury that has breached the intestines and colon and gone untreated for a week is almost always fatal. The infection from the leaking intestines and breached colon had spread throughout Dad's abdomen, and the only way a person can possibly recover from such a condition is to experience a miracle!

Following surgery the doctor said, "If that tree had hit you an inch further to the left or an inch further to the right from where it did, you would have been a dead man." Even so, the colon and intestines had been crushed severely. Because of the severity of the injuries, half of Dad's colon and intestines had to be removed. The tree had fractured the ball joint on his right hip as well, so the doctor set it. I must say that my dad looked like a mummy, wrapped in splints and bandages, when we first saw him.

Mom went back to Phillipsville and found someone to move the mobile home to Garberville so we all could be close to the hospital. The full attention of our family was on prayer and visitation. "I don't know exactly where the turning point came," Dad says. "I just knew I began healing very quickly. I think the Lord wanted me to realize how bad my injuries were, and once I knew, my body began healing supernaturally. He literally pulled me out of the jaws of death once again."

Despite being mangled and torn, waiting seven days for surgery as gangrene took over his abdomen, and lying on a broken hip that was unset, Dad found new energy after the operation. Within two weeks, an amazingly short span of time for such injuries, he was up on his feet, propelling himself down the hospital corridor on crutches.

"My back continued to hurt," he says. "We never found out what was wrong with it. Miraculously the X-rays showed it wasn't broken, but we never discovered the cause of the pain." Incidentally he lived with constant back pain for several years.

At the end of the second week, he was standing on his feet, propped up by crutches, when the doctor came by on his daily rounds.

"I want to go home," Dad told the doctor.

"Do you think you can?" the doctor asked.

"I think I can. Esther has moved the mobile home nearby; if I need help, I'll be close" he replied.

It was done. Three weeks after the near-fatal accident, two weeks after major surgery, Dad walked out of the hospital with the help of a set of crutches. He was grateful to be out in the sunshine that August day and glad to be alive.

For the next five years other complications followed. He returned to the hospital with stomach ulcers. The insurance company sent him to several hospitals, including one in San Francisco, where doctors examined his stomach and colon, and where he received physical therapy for his hip.

Everywhere he went, he heard the same thing: "You're a miracle. You are lucky to be alive."

"No one had to tell me, of course," Dad says, "but every time I heard it from a doctor, I understood what a miracle God had done for me. I had never experienced a miracle before; now I certainly had firsthand knowledge that I could share with others."

The miracle did indeed change the course of his life. After sixty-two days in hospitals across northern California and three years off work, Dad took us all back to Arkansas, where he began pastoring a small church in the tiny town of Bellville. Because the salary was so small, he went to vocational school and learned how to build cabinets and construct homes. In the ensuing fifty years as a bi-vocational pastor, he says that through his construction business he has "literally built hundreds of homes." Because he has always been a bi-vocational pastor, while he was building houses he also helped rebuild hundreds of lives.

"As I look back, my life would never have accomplished what it has had it not been for that day on the mountain of northern California," he says. "It changed my thinking about why I am here, and it gave me a new desire to do something for God. God dealt with me about pastoring and gave me the grace to do it."

In a sense it was "no pain, no gain." Dad tells others that everything we experience has meaning to God. "He even uses the painful experiences of our lives to get us where He wants us to be. Certainly that's what He did with me, and I have never been the same."

My dad, my mom, my sisters, and I have lived long enough to understand why we are to "give thanks in all things." We also know that God has planned our lives through pleasant places, but the journey will intersect with some treacherous terrain along the way. Whether we are in a pleasant place or on treacherous terrain, we will "give thanks" because we know "this is the will of God for us." If we are faithful in the good and the bad times, I am confident God will turn all things to our benefit.

If you find yourself traversing treacherous terrain today, I encourage you to give thanks and believe God to work it out for your and His good. Would you pray the following prayer with me?

> *Father, I do not understand what I am going through right now, but You do. Please help my trust in You to pass this test. I confess to You that I am personally powerless against the challenge I face, but I receive Your strength and have decided to act in Your power instead of my own. I believe I am going to come out of this victorious. I know You are not going to let me fail because You have called me to succeed against everything the enemy places in my pathway. I declare that I am going to live and not die because You have called me to do Your work. Because You are my Lord, I am expecting to receive my miracle at any moment. I thank You for the miracle that is in process in my life. I commit to You that I will tell of Your mighty deeds to all who will listen. Thank You for answering my prayer, in Jesus's name. Amen.*

Three

CAN I CARRY THIS CROSS?

*I*N MATTHEW 27 we are introduced to a man named Simon. He begins as an incidental character in this narrative. Scripture is not clear on whether Simon was forced, encouraged, or volunteered to carry the cross of Jesus. On the surface it appears he was not given a choice. But the one thing we know for sure is this: at an unexpected moment in his life he was called upon to carry an unexpected cross.

It was probably curiosity that prompted Simon to attend the kangaroo court that sentenced Jesus to death. I'm sure he did not wake up that morning hoping to carry the Lord's cross to Golgotha. Rather, he was an innocent bystander, prevailed upon to do something he was not intending to do.

Jesus had been weakened from an all-day trial and from beatings that would have killed most men. As a murderous mob headed out of Jerusalem, herding its prisoners toward Golgotha, Jesus collapsed beneath the weight of His own cross. Not to be deterred from their purpose, the Roman soldiers bent on crucifying this innocent man looked about for someone to carry His heavy cross. The Scripture states, "They found a man of Cyrene, Simon by name: him they compelled to bear His cross" (Matt. 27:32, KJV).

The word *compelled* used here comes from the Greek word

aggareuō, meaning "to employ a courier, dispatch a mounted messenger, press into public service."[1]

I doubt Simon was a volunteer for this assignment. Most of us have better things to do than offer to carry a ninety-pound cross up a mountainside. Besides, the tide of public opinion was running so high against Jesus that it might have been suicide to get involved with such a thing. Those opposed to Jesus were out of control. They might have murdered a friendly volunteer just for emphasis' sake.

Most likely Simon was forced to carry an unexpected cross. Most of us have faced unexpected crosses; everyone will eventually be called upon to do so.

We carry an "unexpected cross" when we are forced to deal with something we did not see coming. Certainly there are things we can see while they are still at a distance, and in such a scenario we can make preparations to deal with them in an orderly fashion. Other things take us by surprise, and we are forced to deal with them on a moment-to-moment basis.

Simon found himself doing something he never expected to do. Likewise, a young couple from Friendswood, Texas, found themselves carrying an unexpected cross in the shape of their second child, Andrew, born April 8, 2005, at Women's Hospital of Texas in Houston.

Doug and Audrey Turnbull were excited about having a child at this particular time. Andrew arrived eleven months and twenty-five days after his sister, Rebecca. They were "Irish twins," less than a year apart, as Doug described it.

The pregnancy and delivery all went smoothly. Audrey had a scheduled C-section, and Andrew arrived at five pounds, six ounces, and twenty-one inches long. Parents, grandparents, and friends were elated.

But a mother knows if something is wrong with her newborn

child. The moment she first heard Andrew cry while still in the delivery room, Audrey knew the sound wasn't normal. She made a comment about it, but when no one else spoke up, she did not pursue it any further.

It was another issue a few seconds later that sent everyone scrambling.

Andrew was not "pinking up," a nurse said. She slipped an oxygen mask over Andrew's face to help him breathe. After quickly doing the routine evaluation, the nurse said she was moving the baby to the neonatal intensive care unit (NICU) for observation and additional tests.

The next few hours were a roller coaster. Audrey was admitted to a recovery room; the baby was on another floor; Doug was running between the two. One moment he was told that Andrew's unusual behavior might simply be his adjustment to functioning lungs, so there was no cause for great concern. Another moment he was told the baby needed oxygen to breathe. Something was not right, and Doug knew it. He was asked to stay away from the NICU while tests were being run.

While Audrey recovered from the effects of an epidural, Doug waited in the hallway. The neonatal team came by and explained what they were doing with Andrew and what they were trying to learn. He talked with the pediatrician too.

As afternoon faded into evening, Doug was told a cardio specialist from Texas Children's Hospital was en route to give Andrew an echocardiogram. Doctors wanted to know how well Andrew's heart and lungs were functioning.

The test was done in the early hours of April 9. Doug, asleep in Audrey's room, was awakened to learn that Andrew's test had lasted more than three hours. Now Andrew was being transferred to nearby Texas Children's Hospital, where his condition could be evaluated and treated by some of the best doctors and equipment in the world.

Moving Andrew to another hospital only five minutes away by ambulance was no small feat. Women's Hospital assigned a special "Kangaroo Team" of attendants to accompany the baby because of concern he would not be able to handle the short trip.

Excitement that had soared so high the evening before had long soured; Doug and Audrey now realized their little boy had a major health challenge and might not pull through.

"I was angered that the doctor took it upon himself to arrange a transfer to another hospital without consulting us, though his actions may have saved Andrew's life," Doug admits. "Andrew's pulmonary function had continued spiraling downward. We asked that they wait to move Andrew until Audrey was able to see him. She had not even seen him since giving birth, and we understood she may not have that chance again."

The hospital "held the doors" until Audrey and Doug managed to get to the NICU. Audrey had one minute with Andrew; then the Kangaroo Team of five explained they needed to move quickly. A pediatric heart specialist at Texas Children's was waiting for Andrew to arrive.

In those few hours life had changed. "I went into planning mode," Doug acknowledges. "I told my mom that all Rebecca's one-year birthday party plans for that Saturday needed to be canceled. The pony ride had to be rescheduled; guests had to be called."

There was little comfort Audrey and Doug could share with each other because neither knew the specifics of the challenges confronting Andrew. Audrey had a double dose of misery. She was coping with the physical discomfort of just giving birth and the pain of not having a baby to hold. She had to stay behind while Doug raced to Texas Children's Hospital to watch over their newborn.

Audrey was released to join her family only when the doctor realized she had to be involved with the decisions affecting her son. She was discharged from Women's Hospital of Texas a few hours later, still on morphine and less than a half-day removed from a C-section.

At Texas Children's Hospital doctors went immediately to work on Andrew. They faced a two-pronged issue: they needed to give him the right medications and put him on the proper machine. Andrew was induced into a coma and paralyzed to keep his little body from struggling. Then doctors decided the most imminent course was to get more oxygen into his blood. Pulmonary hypertension was pushing oxygen out; machines and medications were needed to force it in.

"We learned then the real issues confronting our son," Doug says. "Andrew was born with one lung, and his heart was resting where the missing lung was supposed to be. He had an extra artery that was not helping or hurting him, and he had two arteries that came from the lungs into the heart that were not where they should be. These two arteries were mixing deoxygenated and oxygenated blood together."

Andrew's condition continued to baffle his medical team. When Doug arrived at the NICU in Texas Children's Hospital, Andrew's doctor was "googling" his condition, now being identified as Scimitar Syndrome and later changed to Atypical Scimitar Syndrome. The medical team had to find out about Atypical Scimitar Syndrome because it affected only one in a million babies.

Throughout the hours and countless updates Doug and Audrey needed a way to quantify Andrew's condition so they would know which direction the situation was headed.

"After talking it over with the medical team, we agreed Andrew's birth was a three on our scale," Doug explains. "A 'two' and we would be going home; a 'ten' and Andrew would be going to be with the Lord.

"We saw Andrew rebound several times over the course of several days. We saw a positive result when a medication was increased or a new ventilator was inserted in an attempt to improve Andrew's status."

"At one point they considered putting Andrew on a heart-lung machine, but with no 'exit strategy,' they ruled it out. A day or two later they came back to offer the heart-lung machine strictly out of compassion. Using it might give us more time with Andrew and hopefully gain time for them to figure something out."

There were, to be sure, potential issues with that course of action, which Doug and Audrey discussed with Andrew's team of specialists. "We decided against the heart-lung machine; we decided we were going to put it in God's hands," Doug remembers clearly. "When I looked into the eyes of the head of pediatric heart surgery, I saw a slight nod of agreement, not as a doctor but as a parent. He whispered that it was the right decision. Every time they thought they had Andrew's situation figured out, he would not only worsen but would fall lower than his previous pulse and oxygen levels."

After a few days of staying with Andrew round the clock, the Turnbulls were sent home to rest and spend some time with Rebecca. If Andrew were to pass, they said, the parents would certainly be called so they could have a few hours with him. They were promised they would be able to hold him for the very first time.

So certain did the baby's death seem that Doug and Audrey signed the "do not resuscitate" orders at their doctor's guidance and asked to have Andrew's organs used to help other children. Doug explains, "We wanted someone to benefit in some way from Andrew's short time with us."

Throughout those dark days Doug says he had no anxiety about Andrew dying. "It was more a test of patience and 'wait and see,'" he says. "I know the Word and have been tested several times before in my life, so I knew God was in control. It was more a time of waiting. Because I knew God is wise and good, I knew I could accept life or death. I knew God had a purpose, and if He chose to take Andrew, in time He would heal my heart. I never felt anger at the unknown. I knew God would determine whether Andrew was going to live or die. The predominant question rolling around in our heads seemed to be that, if he lived, would he be able to have a full life without complications?"

Their faith was challenged to the limit on April 12.

Nothing More Could Be Done

In the early afternoon doctors told the parents they did not expect Andrew to last the night. Doug and Audrey were told doctors had tried all the medications available; they had exhausted all options. There was nothing more to be done.

He called me, his pastor, though I was in an important conference with my staff. Doug recalls, "Pastor's words rang out in my mind: 'Is Andrew in immediate and eminent danger of death?' When I answered yes, he said, 'I will assemble the staff and begin to pray for Andrew's healing, and I will be at the hospital as quickly as possible.'"

The compassionate medical team, which had worked so hard for Andrew, told Doug and Audrey to bring in anyone and everyone they wanted to be with them at that point. Family and friends began coming by, peeking in on Andrew and saying prayers. Doug and Audrey joined hands with Audrey's mother and their pastors in the hallway to pray for God's will.

"That's all we wanted," Doug says. "In our hearts we had already offered Andrew to God, but our prayer remained for God's will to be done."

Others prayed as well. Social media, phone trees, and web pages all passed along the word of Andrew's deteriorating condition. Dozens of churches activated prayer chains; hundreds of people reached out to God on behalf of a five-day-old infant who lay at death's door.

"The Word of God sustained us," Doug recalls. "I don't recall a single scripture; Audrey and I would take turns finding and reading one to each other. We felt like Abraham and Isaac; we had been asked to walk up Mount Moriah as one person. We put Andrew on the altar as God commanded and told God to take him if He desired. If He did, we would be blessed with an angel; if He left Andrew with us, we would be blessed with a son. Either way, we asked the Lord that Andrew be whole, without restrictions and limitations."

Love came pouring in to encourage this stricken family. Every morning Andrew's grandpa was at the hospital by seven o'clock to read the Bible to Andrew and pray over him. Doug and Audrey would find time to talk with other families at the hospital, all of them encouraging one another. In the evenings Doug and Audrey headed home to spend time with Rebecca before she went to bed.

Doug recalls a touching moment. "Many mornings after we returned to the hospital, we heard stories from nurses about 'guests' who had stayed by Andrew's side during the night. We learned that one young lady from the Kangaroo Transport Team would stay the night with Andrew and be with him until she was called for duty. We would come in the next morning and find Andrew wrapped with new blankets and new clothes. The staff said the woman found it peaceful just to be with him when she could."

There were milestones of "progress" after prayer. After being stabilized, Andrew had to be taken off paralyzing agents to see if he could tolerate a respirator in his mouth. Then came a gentle effort to get him off the respirator and breathing on his own.

One night Doug received a phone call at home from a nurse

saying that Andrew had actually "pulled the tube out on his own." She reported that the team had let him struggle a short while to see how much breathing he could do on his own. They ended up putting the tube back in, and "he cooperated a bit more after that," the nurse said.

The ultimate test was an MRI to see how much brain damage Andrew had sustained. The question was not "if" but "how much." By God's grace, he received a clean MRI! No brain damage! His condition had quickly changed from "terminal" to "hopeful."

"After Andrew's vitals began to stabilize, we were immediately asked to shred the 'do not resuscitate' paperwork," Doug remembers. "We were surprised at the request and even pushed back at the doctor, saying that it was OK to keep the form on file. But at the doctor's insistence we let him shred the forms."

After Andrew being hospitalized for the first month and twelve days of his life, on May 20, the Turnbulls were told they could take him home! Two days prior Andrew had virtually been given up for dead because his oxygen level had dropped so dangerously low. But the saints barraged heaven with their audacious prayers, and miraculously, without having performed a single surgery on him, Andrew's doctor told Doug the boy was strong enough to go home.

"I knew that day would come soon enough, but to hear the words that he was ready then was a complete shock to me," Doug says. "This was the first time I felt anxious. How could this baby, who had kept busy a team of more than ten doctors and nurses as well as several machines, who had never left the NICU, who had been given some of the strongest medications a baby can take just to stay alive, suddenly be ready to just go home? How could taking him home and letting him sleep on his own be OK?"

But it was true. Doug and Audrey gathered their bundle into their arms and drove home to let him greet his sister, Rebecca.

God had miraculously healed a son born with one lung and a life-threatening pulmonary dysfunction. Why his only lung didn't explode under the pressure it was under, why his oxygen levels stabilized, why he experienced no brain damage, and why the abnormal way his arteries were routed hadn't created new, life-threatening problems could only be due to the hand of God on Andrew's young life.

A VERY SPECIAL FATHER'S DAY

The next few weeks were days of diligence and vigilance. No sick people were allowed into the house. Hands were washed regularly; no one breathed on the baby. Andrew was given every opportunity to gain weight and grow strong.

His first public outing was to go to church on Father's Day 2005. He was presented to friends with ruddy cheeks and a quick smile, perfectly whole. Andrew needed no breathing machines or medications after he was discharged. His recovery exceeded all human expectation.

Today, at seven, Andrew is normal and healthy. He joined a swim team last year and showed no limitations. He loves math and reading and learns quickly. He takes no daily medication and visits the cardiologist on a biannual basis.

Unexpected crosses can take many different paths into our lives. As the Turnbull family discovered, not every unexpected cross looks the same.

Sometimes we are called upon to deal with unexpected crosses in relationships. A family possesses the ability to bring the greatest joy into our lives, but it can also bring bitter disappointment.

At other times we are called upon to face unexpected crosses with our health. When we are healthy, we take our health for granted. None of us ever plan to be sick, but sickness is in the world, and all of us will deal with it sooner or later. And as wonderful as doctors and health care professionals are, they do not have the final word. God has the final say!

Looking forward to the time of Christ, the prophet Isaiah made this declarative statement. "He was wounded for our transgressions, He was bruised for our iniquities; the chastisement for our peace was upon Him, and by His stripes we are healed" (Isa. 53:5).

At other times we face unexpected crosses in our finances. Often, as we are making our way through life, unexpected financial pressure and reversals hit us. These unexpected crosses can come in many shapes and sizes, but our response is in God's Word:

- Budget-breaking circumstances: "The steps of a good man are ordered by the LORD, and He delights in his way. Though he fall, he shall not be utterly cast down; for the LORD upholds him with His hand. I have been young, and now am old; yet I have not seen the righteous forsaken, nor his descendants begging bread" (Ps. 37:23–25).

- Sudden employment changes: "And this same God who takes care of me will supply all your needs from his glorious riches, which have been given to us in Christ Jesus" (Phil. 4:19, NLT).

- Unexpected investment reversals: "Though He slay me, yet will I trust Him" (Job 13:15). Job was given double for his trouble and lived twice as long after the trial than he had before it. He was seventy when his test began, but he lived to be two hundred and ten.

In the face of every unexpected cross I proclaim to you, our source is the Lord! Listen to the words of Jesus:

Therefore I say to you, do not worry about your life, what you will eat; nor about the body, what you will put on. Life is more than food, and the body is more than clothing. Consider the ravens, for they neither sow nor reap, which have neither storehouse nor barn; and God feeds them. Of how much more value are you than the birds? And which of you by worrying can add one cubit to his stature? If you then are not able to do the least, why are you anxious for the rest? Consider the lilies, how they grow: they neither toil nor spin; and yet I say to you, even Solomon in all his glory was not arrayed like one of these. If then God so clothes the grass, which today is in the field and tomorrow is thrown into the oven, how much more will He clothe you, O you of little faith? And do not seek what you should eat or what you should drink, nor have an anxious mind. For all these things the nations of the world seek after, and your Father knows that you need these things. But seek the kingdom of God, and all these things shall be added to you.

—LUKE 12:22–31

Simon found himself doing something he never expected to do. Doug and Audrey Turnbull also found themselves carrying an unexpected cross. Doug and Audrey had no way of knowing what they would be called upon to deal with, nor do we know what we will be called upon to endure. One thing we can be sure of: God will be with us.

At first the unexpected cross Doug and Audrey found themselves carrying was absolutely overwhelming. How could they deal with all the negative reports that were coming at them? Could they carry this cross? They realized the only hope they had was in God. The good news is that God showed up in a big way.

Simon had no way of knowing that he would be called upon to climb a mountain with a ninety-pound cross on his back. But

I believe God stepped in and gave him what he needed to carry this unexpected cross. I am convinced that God gave Simon superhuman strength!

We can also rest assured that no matter what kind of cross we are called upon to carry, God will never allow us to carry it alone. Can you carry this cross? Yes—a thousand times yes! You can do it because He is going to carry the greatest part of the load.

If you are carrying an unexpected cross, pray this prayer with me:

Dear Lord, I never expected to find myself in this situation, but I am here. My strength is depleted, and I ask You to help me bear this burden. I cast my burden on You and give myself to You for Your purpose. I believe Your perfect will is going to be accomplished through my life. I know You as a miracle worker, and I ask You to work a miracle in this situation. Just as You gave Simon strength when he was carrying Jesus's cross and to the Turnbull family when they needed You most, I believe You are now stepping into my situation for the purpose of finalizing my miracle. I give You praise for answered prayer, and I will give all the glory to You, in Jesus's name. Amen.

Four

CAN HE LIVE?

THE STORY OF Jon and Crystal Funderburg reminds me of the account recorded in John 11. Here Scripture spells out the death and resurrection of one of Jesus's closest acquaintances.

Lazarus, Mary, and Martha, three siblings from Bethany, had hosted Jesus and His disciples when they had visited the small village of Bethany, situated on the outskirts of Jerusalem. Other than His earthly family and twelve disciples, Scripture describes no other relationships that were closer to Jesus than the three people mentioned in this story.

Lazarus contracted a sickness that would result in death. As soon as Mary and Martha realized their brother was terminally ill, they called for Jesus to come and heal him. Surprisingly Jesus took His time getting to Bethany; in fact, He did not arrive until Lazarus had been deceased four days.

Jesus's failure to respond to the sisters' request was not taken well! Scripture tells us, "Martha, as soon as she heard that Jesus was coming, went and met him, but Mary was sitting in the house" (v. 20, KJV). Possibly Mary was offended at the way Jesus responded to their requests for help. They had invested heavily into the Lord's ministry and may have thought He should have come quicker. We have all been there, haven't we?

Take a little closer look at Scripture here. Mary was not the

43

only one whose blood pressure had been elevated by the way Jesus responded to Lazarus's illness. "Martha said to Jesus, 'Lord, if You had been here my brother would not have died.'" While Martha goes on to express faith in Jesus, this remark was pointed, indeed. Martha was upset that her friend Jesus had responded so late to their requests for help.

There is a short verse that has been largely overlooked in this passage, and it occurs just prior to Jesus's and His disciples' arrival in Bethany. "Jesus said to them [His disciples] plainly, 'Lazarus is dead. And I am glad for your sakes that I was not there, that you may believe. Nevertheless let us go to him.'"

Here is the real story in this passage: Jesus allowed Lazarus to die! Are you as shocked and offended about this as I am? Why would He do such a thing to a family He had allowed to get so close to Him? The answer is, so He could raise Lazarus from the dead and the faith of all His followers could go to a completely new level!

Often God allows tests so that faith can be developed and our dependence on Him can be taken to a new level. When this occurs and we have passed the test, our ability to produce for His kingdom increases exponentially. God works in audacious ways to build the faith of His people and set us up for future success.

When Lazarus, who had been dead and in the tomb for ninety-six hours, came forth, I guarantee that every single person observing the miracle was forever changed. They never looked at Jesus the same, and their lives and family lines were forever altered for the good!

Not only does God answer audacious prayers, He answers prayers *audaciously* too. Jon Funderburg and his wife, Crystal, were young Christians living in Murfreesboro, Arkansas, when Jon asked God to deepen his faith. After reading Acts 2:2 ("And suddenly there came a sound from heaven as of a rushing, mighty wind," KJV), Jon petitioned God for a "suddenly" experience. He wanted God to let him experience something that would show him the closeness and power of God and ignite him with real faith.

God answered, but not in the way Jon expected! What follows proves that though God may allow us to be tested to the limit of our faith and endurance, He will not allow us to be destroyed. The prophet Jeremiah learned that when a vessel becomes broken, the potter fashions it into another vessel that is fit for use. One thing is certain: when God allows a trial, He always has a higher purpose in mind. If we will not flinch in the fire, we will be "remade" for service and eternity.

Here is Jon's story, as his wife, Crystal, tells it.

In 2006 Jon was thirty-two years old. Our daughter, Aubrey, was four. Jon was settled into a career as a safety technologist/human resources assistant at a saw-mill while I worked with a hospice care provider.

We were young in the Lord. Jon and I had been raised in Christian families but had strayed. When the Lord brought us "home," He set us free from addictions and gave us a deep hunger for more of Him. Many people remarked that Jon must be called to preach because he didn't want to talk about anything but Jesus. Jon's reply was, "God's going to have to knock me over the head for me to know I'm called to preach." He didn't take the call of God to full-time ministry lightly.

It is important to note that Jon had always been in great health. He took a daily pill to treat high blood pressure, but otherwise he was very strong and healthy. He worked out with heavy weights at a gym and did very strenuous work on the family farm. As far as we knew, he had no physical limitations.

Then, on February 2, only weeks before his thirty-third birthday, Jon woke up with flu-like symptoms. He was achy and weak. On a normal morning he would walk outside to feed his horse; that day he couldn't even make it off the back porch. He made his way to a rocking chair and sat down. Getting sick and missing work was rare for Jon, but after a few minutes he realized it was best that he stay home and rest. He called a friend to let everyone at his job know he would not be able to be at work.

Because of the symptoms, we believed Jon had the flu and would recover with a little time and rest. Thinking that, I went on to work.

Sometime during the day his Aunt Sue stopped by to check on Jon. He was so sick that Sue called the local doctor, who agreed to work him into a very busy schedule. We are thankful for Aunt Sue's quick response to Jon's condition. Had she not taken such action, it is likely he would not be alive today.

"HE MIGHT NOT MAKE IT THROUGH THE NIGHT"

Our primary care physician examined Jon and was very concerned by what he saw. Not only was Jon weak, but he was also experiencing abdominal pain that was steadily increasing in intensity. The doctor suspected appendicitis and sent him to the lab for further tests. According to the tests, Jon's white blood cells were extremely high, and the doctor confirmed that there was some kind of significant infection in his body. I was summoned to leave work and drive Jon to the emergency room at St. Joseph's Hospital in Hot Springs, Arkansas, where Jon's appendix could be removed, if necessary.

The hour and a half trip to the hospital proved to be difficult. We stopped several times along the way for Jon to throw up. He seemed to be getting sicker by the minute. By the time we reached Hot Springs at 7:30 p.m.

Jon was vomiting up blood, and his abdominal pain was unbearable.

Immediately the emergency room staff began a series of tests to determine the cause of this problem. To our surprise, appendicitis was quickly ruled out. Other tests were ordered. As the medical team reviewed test results and discussed possible scenarios, Jon grew steadily worse. His pain increased, and the vomiting became more severe.

Lab results showed his cardiac enzymes were elevated and his troponin level was eleven. Troponin is a protein in the bloodstream; an elevated troponin count (as this was) is a strong indication of heart attack. That explains why the doctor on call that evening told me Jon had experienced a heart attack. This diagnosis was a complete surprise because Jon was young and very physically fit. I tried to wrap my thoughts around the test results and the news I was now receiving and found them very difficult to process.

A cardiologist was immediately called in to examine Jon. Once the examination was completed, it was determined Jon had *not* had a heart attack. The cardiologist ordered an echocardiogram, an ultrasound procedure that uses high frequency sound waves to look inside the heart. I watched the process and listened as the technician and physician talked nonchalantly about what they were seeing.

The echocardiogram proved Jon did not have a heart attack but revealed myocarditis, an inflammation of the heart muscle itself, usually caused by a virus attacking the heart. I was told the ejection fraction, or the volume of blood being pumped through Jon's heart, was between 10 and 15 percent. In a normal heart the rate would be 70 percent. Less than 20 percent was considered terminal and a reason to admit the patient to hospice care. As a hospice social worker who understood the terms, I was stunned.

"You must know," the cardiologist told me, "that your husband's heart might stop beating at any time. He might not make it through the night."

Even though the cardiologist had already diagnosed Jon's condition as myocarditis, to cover all the bases he ordered a heart catheterization. Sometime before midnight Jon went into surgery to have a catheter inserted onto the wall of his heart.

The man who returned from the surgical unit looked like a corpse embalmed and lying in a casket. Jon's color was gone; his eyes were closed; he had no movement. My heart was gripped with fear because it was obvious Jon was dying! I had seen the faces of dying people too many times before not to recognize what I saw. From the time we had answered the alarm clock at six that morning until midnight, my husband had deteriorated from a strong, energetic, happy father and husband to a near lifeless corpse. It was too much for me to handle.

Thankfully Jon's dad arrived at the hospital, and we joined hands by Jon's bed in the intensive care unit and bombarded heaven with our prayers. Nurses worked feverishly around us to make Jon comfortable, but we didn't move. We stayed by his side. We prayed audacious prayers in the Spirit, and we prayed with our understanding. We were desperate to connect with God for a miracle of biblical proportions! I am a very normal person; I admit wondering if I would soon be making funeral arrangements, but I also knew this problem was not too great for God. While I was trying to stand in faith, I was also battling fear and unbelief. After all, the doctor had said Jon would likely not live through the night, and wasn't the doctor an expert in these things?

By morning Jon was still with us, but his heart was so damaged he was given very little hope. A nephrologist was called in to address renal failure caused by the issues with his heart. Jon was producing very little urine, and as a result, his kidneys were in crisis. Later he was wheeled down the hall for a second echocardiogram to see if his ejection fraction had improved. Much to my dismay, it had not! I asked when he would have another echocardiogram and was told "maybe in eight weeks." It was the cardiologist's way of telling me Jon was not expected to improve. Every shred of bad news pushed me to a new low; I found myself clinging to faith for this situation.

The next few days were very dark ones. At night Jon would get extremely confused, ripping out IVs and tubes. A physical therapist dropped in to see if Jon could stand up. He could not. In fact, he had gained so much fluid that he could barely turn himself in bed. The incision on his leg, created for the heart catheter, was now pouring out fluid like a fountain. A nurse taped a bag to the site in an attempt to catch the flow of the fluid.

However, despite his mental confusion, Jon still talked about the Lord. It was as if he was confused about everything but God. I could tell his heart and mind had "zeroed in" on the only One who could help him, and his confidence was high. His faith through the whole thing was absolutely amazing.

On the other hand, I was reeling from the constant flood of negative reports. I was told Jon would not survive, and yet, if he did survive, he would be disabled for the rest of his life. I was told his prognosis was terminal without a heart transplant.

COMPLETE AND TOTAL HEALING—NOTHING LESS

As you might imagine, news spread quickly. Jon's ordeal was a big topic at the sawmill and in our church, as well as in our small town and adjoining communities. Everyone who knew us was concerned. Our church consists of a group of people who believe strongly in the power of prayer; in fact, they are a group of audacious prayer warriors. They launched into fervent prayer for

Jon. Prayer chains were activated throughout the region. Prayer automatically becomes more fervent for intercessors when it appears there is no hope from any other source apart from an all-powerful God. Our petition was a simple one: we were asking God for Jon's total and complete healing, nothing less.

Back home, my mother, brother-in-law, and Jon's dad and stepmother all took turns keeping our daughter, Aubrey. I had no worries there. Nor did I think about how much Jon's treatment was costing. Everything was happening too quickly, and each medical test and procedure was critical to his survival. We had health insurance and some accumulated medical leave, but I was certainly aware that we would owe a great deal of money when this ordeal was over, no matter how it turned out. I coped with these issues by telling myself I would deal with money issues later. I was taking one step, one day, at a time.

I'm thankful I didn't have to stay with Jon by myself. His dad was a lifesaver. We alternated sitting with Jon through the night during our stay at St. Joseph's.

Friends and family members began dropping by to see us. I could sense from the look on their faces they realized Jon's chances were slim. My sister told me she truly didn't understand how serious the situation was until she arrived at the hospital and saw so many people waiting to pay their respects. She made a comment that she would return later for a visit but was told, "You better go back there and see him now while you have the chance."

As the days passed, miraculously Jon continued to cling to life. On Thursday, February 9, he was transferred to Baptist Medical Center in Little Rock to await a heart transplant. Jon was now so weak he could not turn himself in bed at all. His body had accumulated fifty pounds of excess fluid. The cardiologist set a goal to reduce fluid by one or two pounds per day. Nothing "curative" could be done at this point, the doctor said. The plan was to reduce the fluid and manage the symptoms while Jon waited to be evaluated by the transplant team.

The next day, however, brought something remarkable. It was as if we had punched a "reset" button and everything was different! Jon's mind seemed to clear, and to my amazement, he told me he was going to get up and go to the bathroom.

"You can't walk to the bathroom, Jon," I said. "You'll fall."

He proved me wrong and astounded us all! Just walking to the bathroom was impossible twelve hours earlier.

Over the weekend he made steady advancements. Between that Friday and Sunday he lost forty-eight pounds of excess fluid. His body dumped fluids so quickly he was taken off all diuretics. His heart began to work well enough to flush his kidneys, and he urinated very frequently all weekend. This was nothing less than a touch from an audacious God!

The cardiologist came in on Monday, astonished, and ordered another echocardiogram to see what was going on. After the test he said, "I had to go back and look at the echocardiogram from last week because this doesn't even look like the same heart! Jon's ejection fraction has jumped to 50 percent!"

"Praise God!" I said.

"Well, that's who did this," the doctor replied.

The next day he told me Jon's improvement "was nothing short of a miracle." Even so, he wanted to observe him a few more days. Those days passed quickly and without complications. Jon was discharged to go home on Wednesday, a day before his thirty-third birthday.

As we drove away, I turned to my husband and said, "If we don't know now that we are in the palm

of the Lord's hand, we will never know it." We felt surrounded by His power, His protection, and His love.
And we knew He had a purpose in all He had done.

The entire family was at our home to greet him. Jon
was the man of the hour! Around town people seemed
to understand that God had answered our cries for help.
We shed many tears of happiness and praise.

As best we could, we made Jon take it easy for the
first week or so because we didn't want him to overdo
it and perhaps have a setback. Yet his strength and
stamina returned quickly, and within a couple of weeks
of discharge from the hospital, Jon was doing what he
loved to do: he was out riding his horse.

In May, three months after his ordeal, Jon returned to
see the doctor. He conducted another echocardiogram
and said Jon's ejection fraction was now a perfect 70
percent. Jon went home to help load a hundred square
bales of hay onto two trailers, and then unloaded every
one of them by himself and stacked them ceiling high
in the shop.

Since then he has required no heart medications at all.
In fact, prior to the incident, he had been on high blood
pressure medication for five years, but God healed him
so perfectly that his blood pressure is normal too! He
doesn't even require a low-sodium diet.

Was all this the result of Jon's "suddenly" prayer? I
believe it was! If we ask God to increase our faith, He
will do it—but He may use very dramatic means to do
so. I believe Jon experienced an event that challenged
His understanding of God and allowed God to show
Himself strong on behalf of His child. Realizing that
He was with us through every step, holding on to us,
changed us in ways we cannot explain. He is dearer to
us now than ever before.

A year later, in 2007, on the exact anniversary of his
healing, the Holy Spirit moved on Jon's heart, and he
surrendered to a call to preach. He was ordained in

2012. Today we are the lead pastors of Harvest Time Assembly of God in Murfreesboro, Arkansas. Without question, God answered the audacious prayers of His people and changed the "altitude" of Jon Funderburg's heart and the direction of his life.

We give the Lord all the praise and all the glory for what He has done, and for every breath we are blessed to take.

∾

THERE'S NOTHING GOD CAN'T HANDLE

In many ways the story in Bethany intersects with this story from Murfreesboro, Arkansas. Because Lazarus had been dead for four days, Mary and Martha no doubt felt Jesus's presence at the tomb was too little, too late. They would have preferred His presence in the beginning of their ordeal, not four days after their brother's death, and they were more than a little upset.

In every situation we face, we must remember that God does not always handle things according to the way we have planned for Him to handle it, nor does He work according to our time restraints. The truth is, had Jesus responded immediately to the sisters from Bethany, they would have gone on knowing He was the healer, but they would never have known Him as the resurrection.

I am sure Jon and Crystal would have preferred a healing on the first day, but if they had received what they desired most, they would never have known Him in the way that they currently know Him. While they never doubted Him to be healer, they now have personal proof that there is nothing too hard for God! God knew before the sudden sickness that He was going to call them to be pastors. Because of what they went through, they will be utilized at a different level when ministering to individuals who are walking through difficult times. They can say for a fact that they know on a very personal level that there is no dilemma that God cannot handle.

The takeaway from this outstanding testimony is that when things are as bad as they can possibly be, never discount the audacity of prayer or the change of direction and condition that can be produced through one of God's "sudden" moments!

If you are in need of a miracle, please repeat the following prayer:

> *Dear Lord Jesus, I approach You today believing that You can do anything. There is nothing that is impossible for You, and all things are possible to those who believe. Lord, I express to You that I believe! The situation I bring to You right now looks impossible from a human perspective. I choose not to allow facts to cloud my God-view of what the Word says I have a right to receive from You. I commit this impossible situation to You and ask that You provide a miracle. I believe the miracle is currently in the making, and I am awaiting its revelation in my life. I praise You in advance for the miracle I am about to receive, in Jesus's name. Amen.*

Five

IS THIS A DEATH SENTENCE?

*N*OWHERE IN THE Word of God are we promised the Christian life will be easy. I realize that there is an "easy listening" gospel afoot in our culture that says if one is in the will of God, everything will work smoothly.

But look at the heroes of faith, and you will discover something completely different. They suffered. They were oppressed. They trusted God and persisted through their trials until victory came. What makes us think we are to have an easier road than they did?

All one must do is look through the annals of human history to conclude that no one gets a free pass in life. Jesus said as much: "These things I have spoken to you, that in Me you may have peace. In the world you will have tribulation; but be of good cheer, I have overcome the world" (John 16:33).

Life provides many surprises we do not understand, yet we know God is in charge of our futures. The only human being who has the power to keep us from the destiny God has set for us is the person who has received the destiny from God! Therefore, we cannot blame our failures or defeats on anyone else. On the other hand, we can rest in the fact that if God said it, that settles it! In such a scenario all we have to do is to follow the prescribed path to victory. Our victory is His victory!

The following story reminds me of the death sentence pronounced upon Hezekiah, the king of Judah. Hezekiah was the son of a king; he began his reign at the tender age of twenty-five. He ruled for twenty-nine years and did what was right in the sight of the Lord. During his reign Hezekiah brought the nation of Judah back to worshipping Jehovah and renounced all other gods.

His track record was stellar, but at the age of thirty-nine Hezekiah developed a health problem so severe that the prophet Isaiah spoke a death sentence over his life. "In those days Hezekiah was sick and near death. And Isaiah the prophet, the son of Amoz, went to him and said to him, 'Thus says the LORD: "Set your house in order, for you shall die, and not live"'" (2 Kings 20:1).

For a thirty-nine-year-old who has everything to live for, this prophecy is not what one wants to hear. We know the news was devastating to this young king because his response was as follows: "Then he turned his face toward the wall, and prayed to the LORD, saying, 'Remember now, O LORD, I pray, how I have walked before You in truth and with a loyal heart, and have done what was good in Your sight.' And Hezekiah wept bitterly" (vv. 2–3).

From the very beginning of the crisis Hezekiah was determined not to take the news of his terminal medical condition lying down! He made a quick and consequential decision to fight for life—and that he did. It appears he attempted to call in some markers of what he had done to turn the nation back to God. We all know nothing we do can earn us a miracle or another day on this planet. God does not trade out favors; what He responds to is a broken heart, a desperate cry, and a faith-filled spirit.

The person who attempts to obtain a miracle from God on the basis of personal accomplishments will walk away sadly disappointed. Such a mind-set says, "God is in debt to me." If we attempt to obtain favors from the Lord on this basis, all He has to do is remind us of our salvation. The miracle of salvation outweighs all we could ever do for God, no matter how gifted we might be.

Sometimes our miracle is a while in the making; at other times it comes to pass immediately! In Hezekiah's case the answer took three days.

> And it happened, before Isaiah had gone out into the middle court, that the word of the LORD came to him, saying, "Return and tell Hezekiah the leader of My people, 'Thus says the LORD, the God of David your father: "I have heard your prayer, I have seen your tears; surely I will heal you. On the third day you shall go up to the house of the LORD. And I will add to your days fifteen years. I will deliver you and this city from the hand of the king of Assyria; and I will defend this city for My own sake, and for the sake of My servant David."'"
>
> —2 KINGS 20:4–6

Notice, when Isaiah returned for the second word, there was no mention of Hezekiah's accomplishments. "Thus says the Lord, the God of David your father: 'I have heard your prayer, I have seen your tears; surely I will heal you. On the third day you shall go up to the house of the LORD. And I will add to your days fifteen years.'" I think you will see similarities between the situation where Hezekiah found himself and those in our next story.

At age thirty-three Rev. William Alvin (WA) Berg and his wife, OcaDean, learned firsthand how tenuous each day can be and how much they must rely on God to see them through. They knew well the truth of Lamentations 3:22: "Through the LORD's mercies we are not consumed, because His compassions fail not."

Their young daughter Diane was ten when the symptoms of leukemia first appeared. She bruised easily, her nose bled for no apparent reason, she had no appetite, and her weight loss became startling. The lymph nodes under her arms and behind her ears were visibly swollen. These symptoms were very disconcerting to this young family.

Day after day Diane battled for life, enduring a host of blood transfusions and a painful blood marrow test. Day after day the family agonized and prayed, crying out to God for a miracle of healing and for the brutal results of this horrible disease to be reversed. As a young pastor, WA sought God and took additional jobs to pay the medical bills while his wife put a protective canopy around her daughter. Since Diane's blood did not clot normally, rough games and activities were out of the question. The life of a normal little girl seemed out of reach for young Diane.

WA and OcaDean, as well as Diane's two sisters, Scharlette and Alvine, grabbed God's hand by faith and never let go. WA preached and believed in divine healing, so the faith of this family was anchored in the Word. They were believing God for a miracle. Their faith was tested many times along the way, but they never wavered.

At the start doctors said Diane had only three to six months to live, but the months passed and Diane survived. Diane's mom and dad fasted and prayed regularly, crying out to God for a healing that seemingly would never come.

What does a parent feel when a child suffers? How are parents supposed to react as they watch their child's life ebbing away? The Bergs chose to place the weight of their concerns upon the Lord, trusting in His goodness and waiting for Him to reveal His will.

Diane lasted three years from the first diagnosis. Her faith remained strong until the end. Though perpetually ill, she never relinquished a child's love of life and hopes for the future. She clung to the belief that with the help of the Lord and the assistance of her loving family, she would beat the horrible disease that had emaciated her frail, teenage frame.

Eventually, though, the cancer cells in her bloodstream ate through an artery in her stomach, and she hemorrhaged to death. Her passing was quiet; providentially Diane had slipped into a coma as the end drew near. She went peacefully into the arms of her Lord, where she would never know another sick day!

Before her passing, Diane was in the yard helping her mother plant flower seeds when she made a statement of faith that would become a guiding principle for the entire family in the decades to follow. She said, "After planting seeds that appear to be dead, and watching the resurrection power of Jesus Christ bring them to life, how could I ever fear death?"

The family was devastated by their loss. It felt as though their prayers had been ignored, that they had lost the fight against the archenemy of their family—death! Feeling her heart could never know anything but a deep and consistent ache, OcaDean could be seen dabbing her eyes with tissue. How could a mother lose her daughter and continue moving forward? She knew life would never be the same without Diane, but she also knew heaven would be sweeter and hold an added attraction for her.

WA struggled to overcome his personal doubts; he discovered it is a very difficult thing for a minister who preaches Christ as healer to lose the battle for one of his children against disease. The enemy screamed at him to give up, but he was stalwart in his faith; he never waved the white flag of surrender. He resolved to continue proclaiming Christ as the healer of the human body, the only true source of improvement for the human condition.

When Diane passed, OcaDena had a dream of Diane running down the streets of heaven beside her grandpa, her hair flying in the breeze.

"I was too young to realize everything that had happened,"

Alvine recalls. "I was sad and upset that my family was crying. We all missed Diane very much."

Though shaken, the family never let go of the hand of God. Step by step each family member cried out in his or her own personal, private pain, and God began to repair their emotions and bring new peace and reassurance. No one could explain why Diane was never healed, but each one testified that God's ways are always best.

"Lord, I'm in Your Hands"

The memories of Diane's sickness and premature death were still fresh when, five years later, the symptoms reappeared, this time in WA, now forty-one years old. He and his family were busy pouring their lives passionately into a new church in Marked Tree, Arkansas, when he began experiencing the symptoms that were far too familiar to the young family.

At the time WA was not only planting a church but also working to supplement his income through a small bargain retail shop he and OcaDean owned in town. God was blessing their efforts in the church as well as in their business. WA was outgoing and upbeat and enjoyed being around people, which made growing a church and business much easier. The business they were engaged in provided many extra opportunities to interact with the community. They were able to share their faith with people they might otherwise never have known.

Other than severe migraine headaches, which were frequent, WA had always enjoyed good health. Then, as had happened with Diane, troubling symptoms appeared suddenly. WA stopped talking, had little energy, and began sleeping and napping for long periods of time, which was very unusual for him.

OcaDean observed her husband's new daily routines for several weeks and realized she had seen the pattern before. She ordered him to make an appointment at a medical clinic in nearby West Memphis, Arkansas.

OcaDean stood beside her husband, holding his hand, as the doctor brought news of the blood tests. "Preacher, you have leukemia," he said. To make matters worse, it was the same type of leukemia that had attacked Diane. The prognosis was terminal.

WA prayed, "Lord, I'm in Your hands." As they sat in the tiny doctor's office in West Memphis, the memory and emotion of Diane's ordeal swept over both of them.

This young ministerial family may have thought they had lost the first round with this disease, but round two was now in full swing, and they were determined that the outcome would be different.

From the clinic WA and OcaDean were sent to nearby Baptist Hospital in Memphis, Tennessee. WA told OcaDean, "Now, Mama, I don't want you crying over this," to which she replied, "I won't—if we can pray the prayer of faith." Grasping each other's hands, they did just that. They decided they would not allow fear to rule the day; they were going to permit faith to get the upper hand. "For God has not given us a spirit of fear, but of power and of love and of a sound mind" (2 Tim. 1:7).

Scharlette came to help during the stay in Baptist Hospital and was horrified to see her father's health spiraling downward. WA's condition became so serious that at times as many as six nurses attended him. While the hospital and medical professionals were performing the tests, WA focused on staying positive and full of faith. According to his testimony, he "never lost the belief that God had heard his cry for help."

Even in his own pain WA gave comfort to others. While he was in the hospital in 1968, the Vietnam War was nearing its most intense point. His doctor entered the room and mentioned he was being summoned to the war zone in a matter of days.

In the midst of his own pain WA reached out to the doctor, prayed for him, and offered words of comfort and assurance. "Remember," he told the doctor, "Hebrews 13:8 says, 'Jesus Christ is the same yesterday, today and forever.'" He utilized this scripture to let the doctor know that the same God who provided protection for him in Memphis would shield and protect him on the battlefields of Vietnam.

WA's condition seemed to be déjà vu. What had taken the life of his child had now seized him. It would have been very easy to succumb to the ravaging effects of this dreaded disease, but Rev. Berg did not intend to give up without a fight.

WA was given round-the-clock care and a regimen of medications, but nothing seemed to help. The more care he was given, the weaker he seemed to become. His energy and appetite completely deserted him, and he lost his desire to talk to or see anyone. This was startling because WA was naturally outgoing, and he loved people. To those who knew him best, his lack of desire to be with people was evidence that his life was slowly slipping away.

WA had helplessly watched his daughter's body become ravaged by this ugly disease before she slipped away into eternity, and the memory of that experience was a constant reminder of his own mortality. The two prevailing issues that were constantly on his mind were what would happen to his family if he allowed this disease to win, and the fact that he had heard from God about establishing a church in Marked Tree, Arkansas. The one thing he was confident of was that his work was not yet finished. Unquestionably his family needed him and the church was growing. People were getting saved and God was being glorified. He desperately wanted to complete the work God had sent him to do.

So, even as he submitted himself to God's will, he prayed audaciously that God would raise him up to finish the work. After all, it was God's work, not his. He believed strongly that God would allow him to continue until the work was complete.

During the most difficult days battling this hellish disease, WA clung to a promise found in Psalm 91:14–16: "Because He has set his love upon Me, therefore I will deliver him; I will set him on high, because he has known My name. He shall call upon Me, and I will answer him; I will be with him in trouble; I will deliver him and honor him. With long life I will satisfy him, and show him My salvation."

The small congregation in Marked Tree began praying round-the-clock, and, as one might guess, word traveled quickly. Pastors and churches all across the state cried out to God that WA would be raised up to provide for his family and finish the work of the Lord.

In Baptist Hospital WA was being treated only for the excruciating migraine headaches he suffered and for an unsettled stomach. By this time doctors had concluded that nothing could be done to fight the leukemia. Because his condition was considered terminal, they tried to make him as comfortable as possible for whatever time he had left. The leukemia, the migraines, and the nausea converged to render him lethargic and in constant pain.

Discouraged, WA prayed, "Lord, I'm willing to come home if You are ready for me, but You sent me to Marked Tree to build a church, and I don't know how to accept allowing the devil to kill me before I accomplish what You sent me to do."

Despite the fact that Diane did not receive her healing, WA's family, church, and friends had the audacity to pray and believe God would raise him up!

"God's Got His Hand on Me"

There was no sounding trumpet or heavenly light announcing a miracle, but one day WA awoke in his hospital bed and realized something was different. OcaDean and Scharlette noticed it too.

He felt alive again. His energy level and appetite returned. He began to walk and talk and entertain his family and visitors. This was nothing short of a miracle. From that point on his condition improved steadily.

"God's got His hand on me," he told his wife. He began to share his feelings of renewed strength with his doctor and nurses. Because the change was gradual, the doctors were cautious but could not deny his improved condition.

From the moment the change began to occur, WA recognized it as divine intervention in an impossible situation. God had come on the scene; his body was healing! Before the doctors and the hospital confirmed his medical reversal, he was praising God and giving Him glory for the miracle to anyone who would listen.

Later, blood tests confirmed what he was feeling in his body and testifying to by faith. Healthy blood cells were multiplying; the cancer was retreating hour by hour! Though he was receiving no chemotherapy or cancer-fighting medications, his body was overwhelming the disease that had attacked him. In response to the audacity of prayer, the miraculous was beginning to manifest.

The improvement was so rapid that by the end of his second week in Baptist Hospital, WA was released to go home. God had completely healed him of all cancer, and in the process had healed him of chronic migraine headaches.

A scripture that became very real to the Berg family goes like this: "He sent His word and healed them, and delivered them from their destructions" (Ps. 107:20).

Today, more than forty years later, WA seldom has headaches at all and has never had another migraine. He lived to see the church in Marked Tree grow and be established. What he learned of God's power and faithfulness through his three-month battle with leukemia he has shared with countless others, strengthening their faith to believe for their own miraculous healing. He has laid his hands on countless people who have themselves received the miraculous.

He and OcaDean have celebrated more than fifty years in ministry, and his work is not yet finished. Now retired at the age of eighty-seven, he resides in Russellville, Arkansas, where he still "fills in" for pastors and churches in the area.

Many times we struggle with our faith because we believe we have heard from God with regard to our miracle, yet it is not manifesting as quickly as we think it should. When Hezekiah cried out to the Lord, his intent was to get a reprieve from the death sentence that had been pronounced upon him. W. A. Berg found himself in a similar situation, wanting to cling to life for the purpose of raising his family and building the kingdom of God. Both men were granted a stay. Hezekiah was granted fifteen years; W. A. Berg has lived almost fifty additional years.

If you find yourself in a desperate struggle between life and death, you should know that as wonderful as the doctors are, their knowledge is limited, and they do not have the final word. God is the giver of life, and it is His sincere desire that we have it "more abundantly." The word *abundantly* means "superior life." It is the will of your heavenly Father that you have superior life in each and every area. I call upon you today not to allow the enemy to run roughshod over you but to stand your ground in God by faith and receive the miracle He has already provided. Declare God's Word by faith. Never stop believing that by His stripes you are healed.

In Hezekiah's situation it took three days for the miracle that had already occurred in the mind of God and had been spoken through the prophet Isaiah to manifest in the natural realm. I encourage you to patiently wait with expectancy until your miracle is manifest in and through you. "You have need of endurance, so that after you have done the will of God, you may receive the promise" (Heb. 10:36).

If you are believing God for a miraculous healing, please pray the following prayer:

> *Dear Lord Jesus, as I come to You, I recognize what the facts are saying to me. Though the reports have not been good, I believe You are God over everything. I confess that You are Lord over sickness and disease, and I declare and decree that You are healing me now. I receive Your healing for my body, my soul, and my spirit. I refuse to allow sickness or disease to overcome me; rather I choose by an act of my will to stand on Your promise for healing. I receive the healing You have provided, and I appropriate it to my life today, in Jesus's name. Amen.*

Six

DO YOU WANT YOUR
STUFF BACK?

*B*EGINNING IN 1 Samuel 27, a very interesting story plays out on the pages of God's Word. David, who was running from King Saul, found a place of safety in the country of the Philistines. David was fleeing to escape the treachery of Saul's jealousy.

Saul had sinned against the Lord, and God had rejected him from being king over Israel. Even though the prophet of God had predicted the demise of his kingdom, Saul continued to reign. The Lord's timing is everything. Just because the Lord has spoken a thing, it does not automatically follow that His word is meant to come to pass immediately.

When the promises of God are delayed, we must exercise extreme patience. We get into trouble when we become anxious. The Bible is full of stories of men and women who received a promise from God, yet because it did not happen when expected, they took matters into their own hands. Abraham and Sarah are a prime example of such impatient actions, which produced Ishmael rather than Isaac. I am sure we can all think of times when we have acted similarly. The result of such actions is never good and almost always impedes the delivery date of the real promise.

David is another example of someone who exhibited impatient

behavior. When Saul was rejected, God sent Samuel to the house of Jesse to anoint a future king. David's older brothers were the obvious picks, but they were not the ones God had chosen. As a last resort David was called from his task of tending sheep into the house of his father, where the prophet anointed him to be Israel's next monarch.

One would assume that David would become king in short order, but the truth is, almost ten years passed before the promise materialized. During this ten-year stretch David passed his time herding sheep and serving Saul. He was a loyal servant, but his gifts were viewed as a threat to the man he was serving. David served with distinction and grew in popularity. The longer David served, the more his talents and public favor threatened Saul, and in time Saul made it his purpose to kill David.

One must remember that on two different occasions during this ten-year period David had the opportunity to kill Saul but refused. David knew better than to touch "God's anointed." He realized that in time God would place him on the throne. Saul was not David's problem; he was God's problem. David had not rejected Saul as king; God had rejected him. David did not anoint himself; God had anointed him.

But even that knowledge didn't prevent David from getting tired of running from Saul. Exhausted, David at one point approached a leader of the Philistines and asked permission to live in his country. That's where we find him in 1 Samuel 27. David was weary and desired a place where he and his men could find asylum. Surprisingly he was granted permission to live in the royal city. Over time David proved he was no threat to Achish, the Philistine king, and was granted permission to relocate to Ziklag.

Ziklag represents a place outside the known will of God. I do not believe God ever intended for David and his men to live there.

The fact is, Saul could not kill David because God had already decided David would be the next king of Israel.

If David had not fled from Saul, is it possible he would have been king much sooner? Ziklag is the path of least resistance.

David didn't stay in Ziklag all the time. He would foray onto Saul's turf routinely, only to return to Ziklag when the pressure was intense. At one point David even agreed to help King Achish fight Saul! The one who had twice spared Saul's life had strayed far from the will of God. When one chooses to live outside the will of God, everything changes.

Look closely at the results of sixteen months of hiding, retreating, self-pity, and living in fear. Ziklag burns! While David and his men were out of town, the city was raided, their stuff was taken, their wives and children were kidnapped, and the city was burned to the ground! Disaster quickly struck David, his men, and their families. Everything had been going along smoothly, and then in one terrible moment, calamity brought devastation as far as the eye could see.

Such was the case in the life of Clint Mayfield. He was twenty-six, newly married, and settled into a wonderful job with Universal Aviation in Pasadena, Texas. He was fun-loving to the core; Clint loved hunting, playing the guitar and drums, working on cars, and playing video games with friends. He was known to drive fast, but on his motorcycle he always wore a helmet and a metal-plated riding jacket.

Those precautions, however, could not protect Clint during a horrific accident on June 13, 2010.

When friend Jerryme and his girlfriend, Loritta, mentioned they were thinking about buying a motorcycle, Clint thought a day-long road trip might help them decide. Jerryme and Loritta rode a rented chopper while Clint took his own bike to make their way to

Shiner, Texas, a small town more than one hundred twenty miles from Houston.

It was a typical, steamy-hot Texas day. At a lunch stop on the return ride, Clint took off his protective jacket and backpack and stored them on the back of his bike beneath the cargo net. Somehow a strap on the backpack worked its way loose a short distance down the highway.

Witnesses say the backpack itself started to slide out of the netting and the strap began flailing. An instant later the strap darted into the spokes of the rear wheel. Instantly the tire was in a bind, not able to spin. At highway speed the back wheel locked up and the bike began to skid down the roadway.

Only Clint's quick reflexes helped keep the bike upright. The bike skidded the length of a football field before the back tire burned through the tread and blew out. It was the force of the blown tire that sent Clint hurtling over the handlebars and into the air. He hit the concrete hard, square on his spine, and slid; the back of his head smashed against the pavement as Clint bounced like a rag doll down the roadway until he landed in a ditch beside the highway more than three hundred feet from where the tire had snagged.

Jerryme said he found Clint lying on his back, slipping in and out of consciousness. Loritta turned on her cell phone and dialed 9-1-1. Within minutes, as Loritta talked with emergency services on the phone, Clint's face turned blue from a lack of oxygen. Jerryme tugged off the helmet to give Clint fresh air, but the rush of cool air made him throw up. Clint wasn't talking and his movements were feeble. He could not speak to describe his condition. All Jerryme could do was stay beside him and give assurance that help was on its way.

In less than half an hour first responders from a nearby town were on the scene with an ambulance. Immediately upon assessing

Clint's injuries, emergency medical technicians decided Clint needed treatment from a trauma center rather than a regular hospital. Since Austin was the nearest city with a trauma center, they called in a Life Flight helicopter and had Clint flown to Brackenridge Hospital.

At home in Pasadena Clint's wife, Andrea, was donning her nurse's uniform and preparing to leave for the evening shift when the phone rang. A man from Clint's company was on the line, asking the name of the hospital Clint had been flown to.

"What?" Andrea asked. "What are you talking about?"

"You haven't heard?" the man asked. "No one has told you? Did you know Clint was in a motorcycle accident earlier this afternoon?"

"No!" Andrea answered, as her pulse suddenly quickened. The other line was beeping in; caller ID said it was Darrell Mayfield, Clint's dad. "Gotta go," she told the man. "I gotta take this call."

Darrell Mayfield didn't mince words. "Clint was in an accident. He's been taken to a hospital in Austin. Grab a couple of things, whatever you'll need for a few days. I'm on my way to pick you up; we're heading to the hospital now."

As the family made its way toward Austin, cell phone calls between relatives already arriving at Brackenridge Hospital began piecing the story together. Clint had entered the emergency room with a Glasgow Coma Scale score of three to four points. The Glasgow Coma Scale is a tool medical professionals use to evaluate a person's degree of consciousness. A "normal" score for people with all senses and reflexes is fifteen; people with a score of eight or less are comatose. The lowest score possible is three. Clint was barely alive.

He had been pushed on a gurney into an MRI chamber immediately upon arrival. There, doctors found multiple subarachnoid hemorrhages (bleeding between the brain and the thin covering of the brain) and cerebral contusions (bruises). Clint's brain stem appeared abnormal, possibly an infarction; his left lung was bruised (most likely aspiration pneumonia); his left ankle was dislocated and swollen; and the C-1 vertebra in his back was broken. Though it went unsaid on the phone, doctors scrambling over Clint in Austin had already concluded his case was hopeless.

The family arrived at nine o'clock and gasped at what they saw. A strong, energetic young man in the prime of life looked broken beyond repair. Clint was bandaged from head to foot. His eyes were swollen and purple. He was intubated, strapped to the bed, and punctured with multiple IVs. He was bleeding from his ears.

Seeing him for the first time, Andrea stood beside him in shock. Softly she stroked his head and whispered into his ear, "I'm here, Clint. I love you."

Clint had been placed into a medically induced coma so his lungs could heal. The next seventy-two hours, the doctor said, would tell "which way he would go."

Visits had to be brief in the ICU.

"The first time I had to leave Clint that night was hard," Andrea recalled. "As soon as we were in the waiting room, I melted into a chair and started crying uncontrollably. I remember thinking that my best friend, the first person I always go to when things get bad, was unreachable. How were we going to get through this? What did this mean long term? I was surrounded by family at the time but felt completely alone."

As a pastor, I am accustomed to receiving unexpected phone calls. But the one I got from the Mayfield family that evening shocked me. My wife, Susan, and I happened to be in Wimberley, Texas, with our family for a few days of much-needed vacation. Wimberley is a couple hours from Austin. As soon as we received the call, we made the drive north to Austin as quickly as we could.

In the car we interceded continually for Clint and Andrea and for the entire Mayfield family. We earnestly asked God to spare the life of this young husband and to heal him from his injuries. At the time, we were not aware just how severe Clint's injuries were, but God knew. We committed Clint's life and future into the Lord's very capable hands.

As I prayed for Clint, the Holy Spirit brought the passage about David's recapture of Ziklag to my mind, especially those words in 1 Samuel 30:8: you shall *"without fail recover all"* (emphasis added). I knew this word, which had invaded my spirit with indefatigable hope, was God's sure word for Clint. No matter what we saw on our arrival, no matter what Clint was up against, I knew he would recover all his faculties and zest for life.

Yet, I confess that what confronted us from that hospital bed was far worse than I had imagined. Seeing Clint so near death, broken beyond human repair, brought tears to my eyes and saddened my heart for this man and his family. I immediately shared with Andrea's and Clint's parents exactly what the Holy Spirit had spoken, and then we gathered in a circle and prayed. The promise of God lifted us! We knew it was His will to heal Clint; we had no need to despair, no matter what report we were handed in the days to come. Heaven had pronounced healing, and healing it would be, even though it might come through a long, arduous process.

WAIT AND SEE

The next morning a neurosurgeon described to the family the various outcomes of traumatic brain injuries. He said it would be very difficult to determine how Clint would be affected; perhaps he would have severe memory loss with permanent loss of bodily functions, or perhaps he would have a minimal loss of memory and his normal functions. It was "wait and see."

Clint was in ICU for two weeks. During that time he remained on a ventilator to let his lungs heal. He was placed on insulin to stabilize his blood sugars, and given substantial doses of Tylenol and antibiotics. Because he had taken off his metal jacket, his back was raw from its scrape on the pavement; he was placed on burn pads to hasten healing and received a blood transfusion. There was a large area, roughly twelve square inches, on his hip that had to be debrided. The skin had to be peeled off so the wound could be cleaned every day. Because the skin had to be stripped away, the doctors were afraid no skin would return without a graft.

Because of the swelling in his brain, doctors inserted an ICP, a small wire that monitors the pressure in the skull. To do so, a surgical team drilled a hole through Clint's skull. The device helped measure any rise in pressure and alerted a nurse of danger.

On the third day, early in the morning, Clint had an MRI that showed his contusions on the temporal (right side) and frontal lobes of the brain. He had a basal skull fracture and his brain was very swollen, but there were no neck fractures.

Clint celebrated his twenty-seventh birthday in a coma, surrounded by his family, who sang "Happy Birthday" to him. Doctors tried to take him off the ventilator after eleven days, but Clint's breathing was still not regular. Instead, he was rolled into surgery for a tracheotomy and feeding tube to be inserted.

About this time the doctor tried lowering his sedation medication so Clint could breathe on his own. Indeed, he opened his eyes and looked about the room. He responded to simple commands such as, "Move your hand." But he was in such pain that he would get very agitated. His ICP pressure would shoot up quickly, and he would be sedated again.

On the thirteenth day after the accident Clint opened his eyes and looked about. Excited by the news, Andrea rushed to his side.

"But I didn't see what I was expecting," she said. "His eyes were open, but they had a glassy look; he moved them around when he heard sounds. His pupils were so dilated I couldn't see the irises of his eyes. I guess I had expected an instant miracle; I thought he would wake up and begin talking to me, as if he was waking from a long nap. When I saw him, I realized this was not going to be an instant miracle. It would take a long, long time.

"So whenever I was alone, I cried a lot. I asked God what lesson I needed to learn because I wanted to learn it fast and pass the test. I thought I truly trusted God with everything, but my fear showed me I did not. In prayer the Lord told me to put Clint completely into His hands. He helped me do so. After that I pictured Clint lying in the gigantic hands of God, resting peacefully."

Later that evening Clint woke up once again and stayed awake awhile. "He saw me!" Andrea recalled. "I went quickly to his bedside, and he tried to grab my hand! He knew me! The nurse released his restraint, and he grabbed my hand with his left hand and put it to his lips and kissed it. His mom asked if he knew who I was, and he shook his head yes! Then he ran his fingers through his hair, something he had a habit of doing before the accident. Those few miniscule reactions told us a major story: Clint was on his way back. God was at work!"

Awake, Clint found himself with a tracheotomy in place, which made it virtually impossible for him to speak. He tried to write what he was thinking but would get frustrated when no one could read what he had said.

Realizing just how much brain function Clint had lost frightened his family. He recognized Andrea but thought they were still dating. The analytical function of the brain was not affected at all, however. Odd, but he could easily remember the numbers on his credit card, his phone, and calculations he performed for his company.

There were other low points during those two weeks in ICU. Needing the tracheotomy was a major setback; the medical team had hoped Clint would be breathing on his own within a few days. Any sudden rise in cranial and blood pressure was dangerous and revealed how precarious his recovery truly was. When despair descended upon the family, they remembered the promise from 1 Samuel: "Without fail, you will recover all."

LITTLE BY LITTLE

Even so, Clint made steady progress. God was at work, indeed. Sixteen days after the accident the doctor said his patient was doing "better than expected" and could start getting ready for rehab. Clint spent the day sitting upright in a recliner beside his bed, trying to talk. His speech was slurred, and his words made little sense, but those who had watched the recovery up close recognized God's promise was unfolding.

On July 4, only twenty-one days after sailing past the handlebars of his motorcycle to strike his back and head on the hard concrete of US Highway 77, Clint was moved to St. Luke's Hospital in Houston. A week later he moved to the Institute of Rehabilitation and Research (TIRR) at Memorial Hermann hospital and began an imposing schedule of occupational therapy, physical therapy, sessions with a neuropsychologist, group therapy, and speech therapy. As always, his wife and parents took turns staying with him. Clint was rarely alone.

The demanding therapy sessions put lots of pressure on Clint's faculties. Often he became reluctant, even resistant. At other times he became paranoid, thinking he was being held a prisoner and police were coming to get him. Or he might suddenly become "hyper-religious," insisting he had to get out of the hospital and find out what God wanted him to do. The push of rehab, though not always easy or pleasant on anyone, helped Clint recover his memory at a faster pace.

Another month and Clint left TIRR for the Transitional Learning Center in Galveston. His therapy sessions continued eight hours a day. During this time no family member could stay with him. The goal was to help Clint become self-sufficient once again. Clint was "trained" in daily living skills such as doing laundry and making a grocery list. He relearned motor skills (such as riding a bike). He had demanding sessions in memory improvement, word finding, staying on topic in a conversation, and other necessary requirements of social interaction.

"His progression—may I say it?—was miraculous!" Andrea exclaimed. "He left full-time rehab to return home on September 15. The man I had seen wrapped in bandages and hooked to monitors and IVs on July 13 sat in his favorite chair in our living room for the first time in three months."

More than just his memory was affected, to be sure. His brain injury had altered Clint's personality and disposition. Before the accident he was rather quiet and would never deliberately hurt anyone's feelings. After the accident he would blurt out anything that came to mind, no matter what it was or whom it hurt. The words might sting, but family and friends were quick to forgive, realizing the loss of brain function. Some things Clint would blurt out were so nonsensical that family members left the room to laugh—no one laughed in front of the patient!

Yes, there was more recovery to be done, more "stuff" to reclaim, but the ground Clint had covered in such a short time was nothing less than phenomenal. He was able to do almost everything for himself except drive. On a few occasions Clint might leave something on the stove to burn, or leave the house and forget where he was going or how to get back, but on the big learning curve, he made visible improvements every day. Little by little, details from the past returned to him.

He went back to work at Universal Aviation in January. His boss had kept his job open for him through the long months and let Clint ease back into his old position as he continued outpatient rehab. Clint passed his driver's test and got his license back. He was getting his life back too.

He was released from outpatient rehab in March. He still had memory problems, so he kept a calendar handy and made written lists. He took naps in the morning and evening, and occasionally had trouble with his balance—and his patience.

Even so, Clint Mayfield can only be described as a living, walking miracle. From that day to this, he has made steady progress, until now, two years after his horrific crash and painful recovery, he has regained his vitality and zest for life as well as almost all of his original mental and physical skills. He and Andrea have a young daughter, Gabrielle Victoria, born after his horrific ordeal.

"Clint has recovered all that the accident stole from him," Andrea proclaimed. "He got back his health, his job, and his sweet sense of humor. And I got my husband back. God did all He promised and more."

Scripture gives us a glimpse into the mood of David and his mighty men on the day of their greatest disaster. David and his men were some of the fiercest warriors the world has ever known, yet they wept until they had no more power to weep. In fact, David's mighty men talked about stoning David. Wow, what role reversals trouble seems to initiate!

"Weeping warriors" seems to be a misnomer, but losses in life can reduce the strongest individual to tears. If your troubles have gotten the best of you, please do not feel you are alone; many have been there. If David and his mighty men and Clint Mayfield faced such a thing, we can be assured that we will not escape.

There are weeping warriors all over the world today; you are not alone! The Lord spoke these words to me: "There is a time for weeping, but this is a time for *faith*."

David immediately did what he knew would work; he went to God in prayer and asked whether he should pursue this band of

Amalekite marauders. Listen to the answer: "Pursue, for you shall surely overtake them and without fail recover all" (1 Sam. 30:8).

In the face of a devastating defeat and an uprising among his own troops, David decided he wanted his stuff back. The most dangerous person on the planet is the individual who has decided he wants his stuff back and is willing to do anything for it! Righteous indignation is an attribute the modern-day church needs to reacquire.

While pursuing this band of criminals, David discovered an Egyptian the raiders had abandoned because he was sick. David fed and restored this man, who, in turn, led David to his enemies. David recovered all.

David got his stuff back! Clint and Andrea Mayfield got their "stuff" back! What are you going to do? What do you need to take back? Please pray this prayer with me:

> *Dear Lord, I have suffered a great loss. The enemy has plundered my life, and I am tired of allowing him to win. You allowed Clint and Andrea and David and his men to have a great victory, and I am ready to receive mine. I renounce everything the enemy has done to tear down my faith. I turn from the self-inflicted, negative decisions I have made that have not been according to Your will. I cast those things down! I lift up the will of God in my life. From this moment forward I will do Your will, and I expect to recover all. I receive Your promise, and I will exercise patience until I see it come to pass. I praise You for Your victory, in Jesus's name. Amen.*

Seven

WOMAN, WHY ARE YOU WEEPING?

$\mathcal{P}$SALM 34:17 DECLARES, "The righteous cry out, and the LORD hears, and delivers them out of all their troubles." Perhaps no cry has more despair than the one of a mother when she learns her child faces certain death.

In Luke 7 Jesus responded to the centurion's faith and healed his son, who was at the point of death. The interesting thing about this particular miracle is that Jesus never arrived at the centurion's home. This Roman commander had sent word that he was not worthy for Jesus to come to his home. He understood authority and recognized the Lord's supreme authority. All Jesus had to do, he said, was speak the word and the miracle would occur.

Sure enough that is precisely what occurred, and Jesus proclaimed the centurion's faith the greatest in the land. I believe what impressed Jesus so much was that the centurion fully grasped the truth that all Jesus had to do was to speak for action to take place. If today's church culture would lay hold of this one detail, we would see miracles on a scale that the world has never before witnessed.

Jesus then traveled to Nain, and upon His arrival was confronted with an intensely sad situation. A widow had lost her only son, and the funeral procession was in full swing. I can only imagine the heartbreak this mother was feeling after losing her only son. If one has any feeling at all, this story stirs the emotions.

The word Jesus spoke to the bereaved mother seems completely off the wall. He said to her: *"Weep not"* (KJV, emphasis added). Can you imagine? This woman's husband was dead, and now she has lost her only son. Then a total stranger interrupts the funeral procession to say, *"Stop crying!"* To ask a mother not to weep in the midst of her son's funeral is like telling a dog not to bark, a rooster not to crow, the sun not to shine, the moon not to glow. Jesus seemed to have asked the impossible of this woman; a mother is going to cry when she loses a child.

What is Jesus doing? He could tell her not to weep because He knew what the final outcome would be. Never forget that He always knows the end from the beginning. He knew death was about to be defeated and the boy would be restored to his mother. And He knows already how He is going to get your miracle to you! His word to you today is, "Quit crying; start believing."

Had you polled the crowd, many would have said Jesus's interruption of this funeral procession was a classless thing to do. The funeral director was probably very upset with this ridiculous disruption to his business. I am sure the family was looking at one another saying, "Someone should do something about this intruder."

What they could not have known was that this was about to be the most unusual funeral they had ever attended. This was going to be the funeral their great-grandchildren would tell their children about! What they were about to witness would fundamentally change the way they looked at death and the way they looked at Jesus.

Read the account as told by Dr. Luke: "Then He came and touched the open coffin, and those who carried him stood still. And He said, 'Young man, I say to you, arise.' So he who was dead sat up and began to speak. And He presented him to his mother" (Luke 7:14–15).

Can you imagine the shock of everyone attending this funeral service? But it was not very long until shock turned to celebration, then complete pandemonium! I am sure this mother's countenance changed from sad to ecstatic! It did not take long for this lady to lose her dignity! Probably she fell at the feet of the Savior worshipping in complete abandonment.

When one receives a miracle of such proportion, concern for public perception quickly fades. Her dead son was alive! She did not care what anyone thought of her; it was time to celebrate!

The widow may have been temporarily caught off guard, but God is never caught off guard. He has an answer for every situation. He specializes in the impossible! Your dilemma may have caught you by surprise, but God is not surprised at all. Before the problem developed, the problem solver planned a path through miracle territory! I challenge you to commit your situation to Him through the audacity of prayer!

God works just as powerfully today as He did during His walk on earth. He is still a God of great compassion and mercy. Here's the story of unborn twins who needed a divine touch, as told by their mother, Evangelina Garza of Houston, Texas.

I was excited at the news that I would have twins. But fourteen weeks into the pregnancy my doctor performed an ultrasound and confronted me with shattering news. The twins, both boys, were suffering from a complication called "twin-to-twin transfusion." The doctor explained that the blood of one twin, Elijah, was passing through to the second, Nehemiah. Elijah was retaining no blood for himself. Consequently he was literally starving to death. In a short space of time this lack of blood supply had caused his tiny body to become stuck to one side of the uterus. He was "shriveling up like a raisin," the doctor said.

If this continued, the prognosis would be bleak. Elijah was gaining barely an ounce of weight each month. At this stage of development he had, we were told, at best a 50 percent chance of survival and a grim 75 percent certainty of mental retardation. Test results, which included a sonogram, confirmed this prognosis.

Nehemiah, on the other hand, had complications because he was receiving too much blood. His tiny heart was oversized and working extremely hard as it struggled to circulate the expanded supply of blood. The doctor diagnosed him with cardiomegaly. His heart valves were not closing properly, which allowed blood to flow back into the heart chamber. The heart had no rest; we were told his heart could give out at any time.

Our doctor sent my husband, Isaias, and me to see a heart specialist at Texas Children's Hospital in the world-famous Houston Medical Center. It was very rare for a woman to have an echocardiogram while carrying a baby in utero, but the doctor wanted us to see for ourselves how sick Nehemiah truly was. Nehemiah's heart was not circulating blood properly. It had leakage and backflow. He was, the cardiologist said, the sickest baby in utero he had ever seen in his life.

In an effort to become as educated as possible and give my babies every chance to live, I agreed to every test the doctors ordered. I saw the bleak results of each test with my own eyes. I spent countless hours grieving and praying over the young lives inside me. There was no explaining why this was happening; I could only cry out to God to help us, to make right anything and everything that had gone so tragically wrong. I asked God not to let my dear unborn sons suffer for something that was beyond their control.

In times like this it is very easy to play the blame game and take on false responsibility. The enemy screams into your ear, "Where is your God now?" Maintaining faith and subduing doubt and fear in complex times is the key to victory, but this is very difficult to do when every word you hear is negative.

"Zero Percent" Chance of Survival

Because Nehemiah's blood flow continued backing up, his heart failed. His body and brain were not getting an ample blood supply despite receiving all of Elijah's blood. Because of this, his organs began to collapse and shut down. By the twentieth week Nehemiah began to bloat as if his body began the process of decomposition. We were told Nehemiah's brain was 95 percent damaged; he was now given a "0 percent" chance of surviving. In the face of such dire news I was a basket case. Emotionally I felt I could not go on; mentally I was completely spent.

The picture being painted for me was absolutely horrifying. Nehemiah had three centimeters of fluid surrounding his brain, causing his face to look deformed. His scalp could not close at his fontanel because of excess fluid.

When we reached this point, the pressure increased for us to terminate the pregnancy. Our doctor wanted us to have a 3-D ultrasound to show us our twins were not normal looking and would be born looking grotesque if the pregnancy continued. He said both boys should be taken at twenty-two weeks. Because this type of ultrasound could not be carried out in the medical center, I would have to fly to Florida for this procedure.

I was determined to give my unborn boys every possible chance for survival. I must confess that I did not dispute what the doctor was seeing. The regular ultrasounds were very revealing, even convincing. I cannot begin to describe my heartbreak as I saw the images again and again, revealing the complications with my unborn twins.

My husband, Isaias, was grasping for hope just as I was. He told the doctor we needed time to decide what we were going to do, knowing the decisions that were to be made would literally be a matter of life and death.

"Time?" the doctor said, obviously upset. "What more proof do you need? I can guarantee you these twins have *no life in them anymore*; it's time to make a decision and let them go."

He wasn't quite right, of course, but he wasn't far off the mark. Elijah was barely holding on to life; I believe to this very day he was holding on for his brother's sake. The doctor said that if Elijah passed, Nehemiah would soon follow. As long as Elijah lived, even though he weighed only a few ounces, Nehemiah had a chance of survival. If Nehemiah died, Elijah would have a chance because he would then keep the blood supply that was flowing through to his twin. The situation was beyond complicated; it seemed the worst situation any parents could possibly face.

In an act of desperation, the doctor recommended we help Elijah by clamping off Nehemiah's umbilical cord. In my mind this was an act of total desperation. Clamping the umbilical cord would stop all oxygen and blood to Nehemiah. Nehemiah would most certainly die, and I would carry one living and one dead fetus until my delivery date. As far as I was concerned, I had not yet heard what I believed to be a viable option.

We were pressed to make the hardest decision of our lives. I cannot begin to describe the anguish we experienced. No matter what we did or decided, one of our boys would more than likely die, and the other would be born deformed and confronted with health challenges that would not only alter our lives but also his from birth to death.

The doctor gave us a week to decide. A week is hardly time to decide on purchasing a home, let alone the future of two unborn children. We prayed earnestly and continually, but nothing seemed to be improving. After being given a deadline for deciding our sons' future, life seemed to go into slow motion and fast forward all at the same time. Every tick of the clock amplified the words of the doctor: "It is time to make a decision and let them go."

Nehemiah's heart was now the size of his chest, and because of amniotic fluid around his heart, abdomen, and lungs, his bladder and kidneys began failing. We knew his life was more fragile by the moment. Our decision was looming before us like a huge funnel cloud from which there was no shelter for protection. We were told very emphatically that he had only one week to live.

The week passed, and remarkably, Nehemiah was still alive! His breathing was not labored, and his movements were normal! The doctor couldn't understand it.

"For sure, Nehemiah is a fighter," he said, "but this baby will be dead in three days or less, *no more.*"

We felt there were some encouraging signs, but we got only discouraging news. We realize the doctors were doing the best they could, delivering a prognosis based on what their education, equipment, and medical science was telling them, but we knew we served a God who could do the impossible.

"I've done all I can do," the doctor said. "If you don't go to Florida, I can't see you anymore. The risk to you in continuing this pregnancy is too high and complicated."

That's when faith took hold of my husband! He grabbed me by the hand and pulled me up from the ultrasound table.

"Let's go!" he said.

"What are you doing?" said the doctor. "Where are you going?"

"Thank you, doctor," Isaias said, "but we are not killing our babies. If God wants them to die, He will have to do it Himself."

The doctor said, "If you think your twins will make it, then you're wrong. It will take a miracle for them to survive, and I've never seen a miracle in my entire medical career."

Isaias squared his shoulders. "Doctor, we might lose our boys, but we still trust in the Lord. Our God performs miracles!" We walked out the door as the doctor stared in disbelief.

"What Do You Want From Us, Lord?"

Once outside I began sobbing. I wanted to fall to my knees. I felt completely helpless and spent. It appeared to me that we were losing the fight, and I had no answers. I didn't know where to turn or what to do next. In retrospect I realize that when we come to the end of ourselves, God can do His best work. He intervenes in a way so no one else can take the credit!

All I could do was pull myself together, accept our decision to "walk things out," and let God decide who was to live and who was to die.

I cried out, "What do You want from us, Lord? What can I do? I'm in need of You and Your healing hands. Please don't turn Your back on us." I shouted at heaven, "Didn't You hear the doctor say that unless a miracle happens, they won't survive? Prove him wrong, Lord! Show him what You alone can do! Please don't let us down."

As I now know, desperation is the raw material for the making of a miracle. We cried the entire drive home, praying in the Spirit and sobbing out loud. I have never known such intense anguish in my life!

That very Sunday night our church, CT Church in Houston, Texas, was having a "miracle and healing service." We decided to attend and believe God for a miracle of epic proportions. The service began with compelling worship, then a faith-building message was spoken from the Word of God. The remainder of the service was devoted to an extended time of prayer for specific needs.

That night a dear friend, Kim, took my hands and prayed with me, agreeing in faith that God was going to bring both boys through this ordeal, and they would live and not die. We prayed that Elijah and Nehemiah would be perfectly whole, despite the overwhelming evidence to the contrary.

Kim told me to write the date on a piece of paper and carry it with me so I would remember the day God healed my twins. I cannot begin to describe what that prayer time did for my faith. The words Kim spoke over me were the first positive words I had received in weeks! I did, in fact, write the date down; the day was Sunday, November 2, 2003.

We went back to the doctor the following Wednesday. I was very nervous because I was not sure how the doctor would respond to us. He was pleasant and sympathetic, and he performed another ultrasound.

As he worked the instruments, he said, "Here goes Baby B [Nehemiah]." He looked around and said it again: "Here goes Baby B." Then an unmistakable look of confusion crossed his face. "Unbelievable," he said. A few seconds later he said it again, but with more emotion: "Unbelievable!"

Nehemiah's heart had shrunk to its normal size! There was still evidence of fluid around his brain, but his organs were functioning and there was little sign of sickness! Praise God! The doctor seemed stunned. He looked completely flabbergasted! My eyes were brimming with tears, and I whispered, *"God!"*

From the evening of the "miracle and healing service," the twins improved every single day. I was admitted to the hospital at week twenty-nine and stayed until my delivery date five weeks later.

Before delivery our doctor attempted to prepare us for the worst by telling us Nehemiah would more than likely take a first breath and expire due to exhaustion from the sickness. He said Elijah possibly would live. He ordered the neonatal intensive care unit (NICU) team to stand by in the delivery room just in case.

On February 2, 2004, the babies were born. They cried like normal babies cry and from the outset began breathing on their own! We were ecstatic!

As soon as the twins were delivered, the doctor asked a nurse to bring him a carton of milk and syringes. He placed my placenta on the surgery table and began injecting the vessels with milk to see which veins were clogged and how the sickness might have happened.

Isaias was videotaping the boys in the nursery when the doctor sent for him. He wanted Isaias to record him injecting the placenta.

We still have the video of the doctor showing us the placenta. He pointed out where blood vessels from the two boys intersected, which allowed Elijah's blood to move into Nehemiah. Then he showed us where the vessels "clogged up," which returned the blood flow to normal for both boys.

"It's a miracle," he said. "These blood vessels clogged up on their own as if performed by laser surgery." He told us no doctor would ever see such a thing. He was very clear that there was "no sign pointing to how the sickness began, but there is evidence how it ended. We will never know how it happened."

He may never know how it happened, but we know God performed His own supernatural surgery and healed our twins. When Doctor Jesus performs a surgery, He doesn't need an operating room, a surgeon's scalpel, anesthesia, or any other conventional thing. He just does His precise, laser surgery with His Word!

The doctor said Nehemiah would spend half his life having ultrasounds and echocardiograms in Texas Children's Hospital, but this prediction too proved to be completely wrong.

I took Nehemiah to his first follow-up appointment on March 31, 2004. The report that came back showed his heart was completely normal; he had the heart of a normal baby! He had no more need of echocardiograms. Both boys are perfectly healthy.

From beginning to end this miracle had the fingerprints of God on it. He performed the whole thing on His own! He is a God who hears and answers prayer!

We began this chapter relating the story of Jesus raising a widow's son from the dead. As far as I am concerned, Isaias and Evangelina's sons, Elijah and Nehemiah, were raised from the dead. This miracle occurred in response to the audacity of prayer and believing God is bigger than the report of a doctor!

No doubt the doctor in this story was doing what his education and experience told him to do, but God did what His Word called for Him to do! When we place ourselves in position to allow Him to do what His Word calls for Him to do, we can get ready for a miracle because one is on the way!

Sometimes we are guilty of being driven by facts when the highest form of reality is what God's Word has to say on the subject. I challenge you to stop being driven by the word being spoken over you by people, even professionals, and rivet your faith to a God who still brings miracles into the lives of those who dare to believe Him. Human help is good to a point; all knowledge comes from God, and there is certainly nothing wrong with accessing that knowledge. But mistakes are made when we release the hand of God and grasp the hand of human help exclusively. We should acknowledge facts, then turn our attention to the One who spoke the world into existence.

If you are facing an impossible situation, I encourage you to pray the following prayer over your life:

Dear Lord Jesus, I acknowledge the facts in my life. I am in need of a miracle, and the human help around me is incapable of creating one in my life. I am fully aware that I am powerless to affect a change in my situation. I release my situation to You and ask for a miracle to occur that will defy all logic. Since I have given this to You, I no longer own it; You do. I will expectantly await the good news that You have worked Your will in this matter. When the miracle that has already happened in the spiritual realm becomes manifest in the natural realm, I will make sure that no one gets any credit or glory but You. Amen.

Now, take time to praise Him for what He is about to do!

Eight

CAN HE CALM A STORM?

ARK 6 RELATES a very famous story of Jesus feeding five thousand men plus their wives and children with five loaves of bread and two fish from a boy's lunch box. This story is known far and wide, as children are taught its details from a very young age. We are not sure how the disciples convinced the little boy to give up his lunch, but in so doing, he became part of one of the great miracles of the Bible.

We can never know when a common action will turn to a miracle, but one thing is for sure: God is able to turn our actions into more than they were intended to be. In fact, God is looking for people who will trust and believe Him to turn their difficulty to good for His name's sake.

Following the miracle of the loaves and fish, Jesus commanded His disciples to get in a boat, cross the sea, and meet Him in Bethsaida. After the disciples boarded the boat, Jesus sent the multitude away and went up into a mountain for a time of communion with the Father. Late in the evening Jesus decided to go to Bethsaida to meet His disciples. They took a ship, but He decided to walk on the water. A violent storm had engulfed the boat so that the boat was in danger of capsizing.

When evening came, the boat was in the middle of the sea;
and He was alone on the land. Then He saw them straining
at rowing, for the wind was against them.

—MARK 6:47–48

We have all been in situations where we struggled for survival
as the prevailing winds of life threatened our very survival. Storms
can take on many faces: family issues, job losses, health challenges,
just to mention a few. No one is exempt from being tested during
our journey through this world that has been blighted by sin.

One of the most shocking aspects of this story is that even
though the disciples were in a struggle for their very lives, verse
48 says Jesus "would have passed them by." Really? He would have
passed them by? Think of it: the passengers in the boat had spent
the day hanging out with Jesus. They were fresh from the miracle
of the loaves and fishes, yet now, only a few hours later, they find
themselves in need of yet another miracle. And when the need for
this latest miracle arises, Jesus would have passed right by them!

This flies in the face of most of what we know and hear
preached from pulpits across America. The game changer here is
the anguished cry of the disciples as Jesus was passing by the boat.
I think the lesson is that God responds to the desperate, faith-filled
cries of His people. Jesus responded to His disciples on the sea,
and God responds to His children in these modern times. Almost
everyone cries out during desperate times, but the thing that got
Jesus's attention was that they cried out to *Him*! Desperate times
call for an all-powerful God!

In January 2011 Johnie and Tiffany Brasher were snuggled com-
fortably into their home as a disastrous tornado approached the
Birmingham, Alabama, area. Even the televised weather forecasts
could not have predicted the destruction that would bear down on
them that infamous night.

On the evening of the storm the young couple was living in their first home, located in Clay, Alabama, on the outskirts of Birmingham. Johnie managed a nearby tire dealership while Tiffany was content to stay home and care for their three-year-old son, Brodie.

January 23 was cold and overcast, which was not unusual in northern Alabama. Gray clouds seemed stitched together from one corner of the sky to the other, and the sky seemed to grow darker by the hour. There was no rain yet, but if the local weather newscaster was correct, atmospheric pressure was dropping, producing the possibility of severe thunderstorms and tornadoes later that evening. Tornadoes in the South are not that uncommon; no one seemed particularly concerned, and people went about their business as they would during any other kind of inclement weather.

The couple was proud of their home, a small, late-1980s foreclosure they had recently purchased and remodeled. They had bought the home at a really good price and with the help of family and friends had performed most of the necessary repairs. The home had three bedrooms, two baths, a large playroom, and a basement; it was situated on an acre of land.

After many grueling weeks of working on their fixer-upper after work and on the weekends, the young couple and son were finally able to move into their new home. By January they had been enjoying the spacious rooms and large yard for almost a year.

Despite tornadoes in the forecast, the family kept their usual evening routine. Johnie, who had to get up very early to go to work, had decided to go to bed early. Tiffany put Brodie to sleep in his room, while she, being a night owl, stayed up late folding clothes and doing household chores that were impossible to do during the day while attending to a toddler.

That night the residents of Clay, Alabama, were awakened at about two thirty in the morning to the sound of tornado sirens piercing the serenity of the night. Tiffany quickly got out of bed, ran to the window, and discovered to her horror that the storm was extremely intense and threatening. It appeared to have them in its sights. The noise of the storm was so loud that it penetrated the windows and walls of their little home. It sounded as if they were standing outside rather than inside despite the doors and windows being securely closed.

Tiffany turned the television on to get an updated weather report from the station in nearby Birmingham. Local radar showed a map streaked with bright red and orange, colors denoting intense thunderstorm activity, and the meteorologist announced a tornado had been detected and a tornado warning was in effect. A tornado watch is forecast when conditions are in place that would allow a tornado to form. A tornado warning is a completely different prediction; this means a tornado is so likely that the weather predictors are watching to see where one develops. The weather forecaster pointed to the area under the most imminent threat, and to Tiffany's dismay the weatherman pointed to the city of Clay and stated it was, in fact, in the direct path of the approaching storm.

Tiffany became alarmed. She quickly roused Johnie from his sleep and alerted him of the situation. They sat on the sofa for a few minutes watching as the storm tracked ever closer to their town and their home.

It was late, but Tiffany knew she could call her parents at any hour. Ricky and Vicki Lee were Alabama natives living and working at a church in Houston, Texas. Having lived in the South their entire lives and along the Gulf Coast for a few years, they knew the danger that hurricanes and tornadoes could impose on the residents in their paths.

In the Center of the Storm

Johnie and Tiffany and Ricky and Vicki Lee were all devout Christians and knew the power of calling out to the Lord when danger was imminent. This family knew how to pray, and that is exactly what they began to do. While talking to her parents, Tiffany switched on the phone's speaker so her parents could hear the newscast.

Everyone involved knew how deadly tornadoes could be because they had witnessed many storms. In fact, a tornado had touched down in Joplin, Missouri, the previous May, cutting a path a mile wide through town and killing one hundred sixty people. This was fresh on the minds of this young family as they found themselves in the direct path of this dangerous storm.

Though they were aware of the danger of their surroundings, they had lived through several tornado watches and warnings before. What were the odds that this storm would come close to their home? They assumed that if a tornado were to actually touch down in the area, the chances were slim it that would approach anywhere near Johnie and Tiffany's house. As with most people, they did not believe the storm would affect their own home and family.

They stayed glued to the newscast and talked about what to do if this was not a false alarm. About that time the meteorologist came on the screen with a very tense announcement: the area predicted for impact had been expanded. The town of Clay sat in the very center of the storm's projected pathway.

Tiffany looked at Johnie, and Johnie looked at Tiffany. They realized it was time to take all necessary precautions.

Over the next fifteen minutes Johnie emptied a closet beneath the stairwell leading to the basement because he believed it would be the safest place in the house for his young family. He took mattresses off beds and put them inside the tiny closet, as Tiffany scooped Brodie out of bed and gathered up needed items for the toddler's backpack. Mother and son then entered the closet and meshed their bodies together against the mattresses; Johnie sat outside the closet on the stairs, listening to the sounds of a storm growing angrier by the minute.

The scene was absolutely terrifying. Tiffany remembers, "I called my parents and sister to let them know where we were and what the news was saying." The entire family was praying, and Tiffany said, "My mother prayed with me right then over the phone and assured us she would continue to pray until the storm passed." Mother and daughter stayed on the phone, praying and listening as the events unfolded in her daughter's home eight hundred miles away from Houston.

Suddenly an inexplicable noise engulfed the house and Tiffany screamed!

"Johnie! Johnie, get in the closet!" Before Johnie could react, the tornado hit like a huge fist from the sky against the house! Windows shattered as ceiling plaster and sheetrock crashed down all through the house. Their ears popped from the changing atmospheric pressure, and Johnie found himself trapped, half in and half outside the closet, unable to muscle himself forward against the wind and the pressure of the storm.

Precisely at the moment of impact, the cell phone went dead. Tiffany recalls, "I remember praying and asking God to keep us safe. I was praying in the spirit when, all of a sudden, Brodie was being pulled from my arms by the suction the storm was creating! I felt that despite all I could do, I was losing him! I begged the Lord not to allow him to be taken from me!"

The house was shaking uncontrollably and seemed ready to crumble. Tiffany locked Brodie between her legs to keep him from being torn from the closet and into the darkness of the storm. In an effort to do all he could to protect his wife and son, Johnie placed his body on top of the two. Still not fully inside the small closet and unable to close the door, he pulled the remaining mattress on top of his family.

"The roar was deafening," Tiffany recalls. "We heard heavy objects hitting the side of the house and could feel a sucking sensation created from the storm; the tornado was trying to suck us out of the closet and out of the house! Our ears popped, glass was flying through the air, the noise was deafening, and the house literally moved from side to side. I pulled the mattress out of Johnie's hand because he was being pulled out of the closet. I felt Brodie literally being lifted out of my arms! All I could think to do was scream and tell Johnie to find something to hold on to."

Though they were separated by many miles, the entire family began to pray audacious, desperate, faith-filled prayers.

Tiffany remembers, "At one point I sensed we were not going to survive this. As soon as that thought entered my mind, I prayed with a boldness I had never known before: I commanded angels to sit on top of the house, and I spoke to the storm. 'Lord, make it stop *now!*'"

From her home in Moody, Alabama, twenty-five miles away, sister Heather was watching the tracking of the storm on television and texting her parents in Houston.

"The storm is hitting them *now*, at this very second!" she wrote.

Miraculously, as soon as Tiffany prayed the words, "Make it stop *now!*" The house *instantly* stopped shaking, and a hush fell over them. Just like that, the storm was gone more quickly than it appeared! What seemed like an eternity had lasted only thirty seconds.

Tiffany's mom said, "I can't describe the feeling that came over us when that phone went dead." She and Ricky prayed fervently in the spirit and with their understanding that God would spare their children. They said they specifically asked God to "put angels over the roof of that home so it would not blow away." They were too far from their children to help them through the storm, but the God they served had experience with storms. He had calmed more than one storm in His Word with a simple phrase, "Peace be still," and they believed He would do it again when they needed it the most!

After a few minutes the phone rang. It was Tiffany, and she was screaming! Everyone had survived; the family was all right, but they were terrified from the experience.

"I was in a state of shock," Tiffany said. Their next-door neighbor kicked down the front door and found them too shocked and stunned to really know what to do. He yelled for them to get up and get out; the house was so badly damaged it was not safe to remain where they were. And another storm was headed their way!

Tiffany remembered, "I grabbed Brodie, and we ran as fast as we could to a neighbor's house. As we crossed the yard, we could smell natural gas; the gas main was broken, and gas fumes were spewing into the air. I knew this could not be good!"

Tiffany continued, "When we reached the house next door, I realized I could use my phone again." In that short time she had missed twenty-seven calls and texts. Their family was terrified about their well-being and was frantically attempting to reestablish contact during the storm.

While racing to the neighbor's home, Johnie and Tiffany looked back at their home and were shocked to see the destruction. Trees were down everywhere. Furniture was strewn on the lawn and onto the streets. Their house had gaping holes in the roof and the sides. Power lines were dangling; the shredded debris made the area look like a war zone.

The tornado had wreaked such havoc on their home the family was forced to stay with friends the remainder of the night. At first light they were back, walking through the ruins of their beautiful home. They were surprised to find it still standing but extremely damaged.

"That moment was almost surreal, like it wasn't really happening," Tiffany said. "To be very honest, all I could think was that God had spared Brodie. My baby had never left my arms."

Though much of the furniture was destroyed, Tiffany quickly discovered blessings in the rubble. Family photos and letters had been spared. Pictures of Brodie had gone untouched by wind or rain, as had their clothes.

Also untouched was Tiffany's piano, given to her as a child. "That piano meant a lot to me," she said.

Tiffany and Johnie found several silver linings in their dark clouds. They were alive and well, and their family had not perished at the hands of the storm. In retrospect all of us can find hope in times of hopelessness even though it may take some time to surface.

As they walked the property, they discovered:

- The entire left side of the basement had been destroyed.

- One column of brick was left to support an entire side of the house.

- The roof had been lifted off and settled back down but was still in place. Both Tiffany and her parents had prayed very specific prayers that God would not allow the roof to blow off the house. Had the roof been taken, there is little doubt that the entire family would have disappeared through the opening.

- Every tree was gone.

- Every shrub had disappeared.

- Brodie's wooden playground set that had been cemented into the ground was nowhere to be found.

- The neighborhood across the road was totally destroyed.

All that, yet the family had made it out alive and without a scratch! They had looked an F-3 tornado, one of the worst possible storms, in the eye and lived to tell about it! To God be the glory!

WHEN TROUBLE TURNS TO TRIUMPH

Because they were well covered with insurance, a month later they moved into a larger, newer home with a full basement. "The storm had damaged our home so badly that it was deemed unfit for habitation," Tiffany acknowledges. "The insurance estimated our losses at well above $200,000. We were given the choice of rebuilding the same floor plan on the same lot or finding another home somewhere else. We decided to take the money and find an existing home."

Tiffany's parents proved to be a great help in the unsettled days immediately following the storm. "My mind was nowhere clear enough to think of things that needed to be done," Tiffany says. "Mom handled everything, from contacting insurance companies to calling storage units to getting us a temporary home and replacing items we needed immediately. Without her, I'm positive our story would not have turned out as happy as it is today."

The blessings of the Lord followed them in those transitional weeks and months of winter and spring. "Our first home was older, with three bedrooms and two small baths. It had a large, level lot. The house we were able to purchase following the storm was only a year old with a full basement, a large garage, and a safe room for storms. It is on a large lot and has four bedrooms, three full baths, a back deck, and small front porch. We love it."

The old house was demolished and the property has been sold. The couple took their insurance money and put it down on the new house. After applying funds from the sale of the lot to the new mortgage, they are now debt-free.

"Prayer works!" the young mother exclaimed. "As soon as I spoke the words, 'Peace be still,' the rain and all the noise stopped. God spared my son and husband that day. He heard the cries of my heart, and I learned that when you are in the middle of a storm, pray!"

The entire experience taught Johnie and Tiffany that God is with them no matter what. They said, "God may allow us to go through hardships which, in the moment, we do not understand. We may question Him; we may even become angry or upset. But He knows our future and sees things we cannot begin to comprehend. Through it all, He will take care of us; He will provide."

"That day, I learned to trust the Lord," Tiffany said. "He was all I had. My very breath. My husband and son were all in His hands. The storm taught me I could trust in His Word."

Tiffany's mom said, "As they were moving into the new house, little Brodie told me he had said, 'Thank You, Jesus, for my new home.' I said, 'That's good, Brodie! It's right to thank Jesus.' Then Brodie said, 'Do you know what Jesus said when I thanked Him, Nan Nan? He said, 'You are welcome!'"

And we are welcome, every single time He provides for us. Johnie, Tiffany, and their family cried out to the Lord in distress, and He heard them. The disciples did the same thing, and Jesus reacted in exactly the same way: "He talked with them and said to them, 'Be of good cheer! It is I; do not be afraid'" (Mark 6:50).

What a comforting statement this must have been to a band of weary disciples after a long day of ministry! They were in the middle of a storm that was threatening their very lives. They were "straining at rowing" when Jesus came to them with a solution to their problem. Now that I think about it, He always seems to show up at exactly the right time with the perfect solution.

Most people overlook the ending statement of this story: "They were greatly amazed in themselves beyond measure, and marveled. For they had not understood about the loaves, because their heart was hardened" (Mark 6:51-52).

This statement clearly communicates the fact that the disciples had not quite grasped the moment or the miracle of the loaves and fish. How could that be? Jesus fed five thousand men plus their wives and children with five loaves and two fish that had been brought to the crusade by a little boy. There may have been upward of twenty thousand people who ate their fill; then the disciples retrieved twelve baskets of fragments!

What is Jesus insinuating here? The inference is that they had just witnessed a miracle that would be talked about for more than two thousand years, yet within a couple of hours they were frightened out of their minds by their latest dilemma. The storm was bigger than their faith.

I believe Jesus was pointing out that their faith had been unaffected by the miracle of the loaves and fish. How could one be afraid of a storm on the heels of such a phenomenal miracle? I'm not sure how such a thing happens, but that is the challenge all of us face when confronted by our latest storm. Are we going to believe God for a miracle or be terrified of the storm?

I trust your faith will be affected by the biblical miracles mentioned in this chapter and the miracle of the hand of God sheltering Johnie, Tiffany, and Brodie from a tornado in 2011. I challenge you to let your faith rise and believe that God is going to come through for you, no matter what your present circumstances seem to be saying.

God is no respecter of persons. What He did with the little boy's lunch; what He did on the sea for His disciples; and what He did for Johnie, Tiffany, and Brodie, He is more than willing and able to do for you! If you are facing a storm in your life, please pray this prayer with me:

Dear Lord Jesus, I am in a storm that is threatening my life. I am personally powerless against this storm, but I believe You walk on water and calm storms with Your Word. I surrender myself to You and Your purposes right now. I relinquish my will to You. I ask You to speak peace to my storm and perform a miracle. I believe that what You did with the little boy's lunch in Mark 6; what You did for the disciples; and what You did for Johnie, Tiffany, and Brodie, You will do for me. I accept Your favor in my life, and I thank You, for I believe You are going to turn my trouble into triumph. When the storm has ended and Your answer has been secured in my life, I will make sure that I share the miracle that ensues with everyone who will listen. I will turn all praise back to You, in Jesus's name, amen.

Nine

ISN'T THAT RIDICULOUS?

REMEMBER THE STORY of Elijah and the poor widow? Because of the sin of the people, the prophet Elijah prophesied to King Ahab that it would not rain on the land until he gave the word. That drought lasted three and a half years. Whether you've experienced drought or not, I'm sure you can imagine how miserable things must have become.

As a result of the drought, Ahab hated Elijah and wanted to kill him. Ahab failed to realize that Elijah was not to blame; sin was the culprit. God was judging the sinfulness of the nation in an attempt to get His people to turn their hearts back to Him.

During the drought God gave Elijah water by the Brook Cherith and sent ravens with bread and flesh in the morning and evening to feed the man of God. In the course of time the brook dried up, and Elijah was forced to move on.

From Cherith, God sent Elijah to Zarephath. There he engaged in a conversation with a widow who was financially destitute. He asked her to cook him something to eat, only to discover that she was gathering wood for a fire so she could cook one last meal for herself and her son. Then, she said, they were going to die. This widow was in no financial position to be entertaining guests; she had only enough food for one final meal, and she had no means of acquiring additional resources.

One might think Elijah would pray for her and move along, but he does something I find to be over the top, out of bounds, even audacious. Knowing her situation, he asked the widow to make him a cake first! If Elijah was a real man of God, he would find a way to help this family rather than requiring them to give him all they possessed, wouldn't he?

There are times in our lives when the path to healing, help, and prosperity is purposely planned through ridiculous territory! All of the great heroes of faith were called upon to do things that seemed to be ridiculous:

1. Abraham was told to go but not told where.

2. Moses was asked to return to a country in which he was a fugitive from justice.

3. David was required to fight a giant with a slingshot and five rocks.

4. The three Hebrew children were told not to bow in worship to someone other than God despite threats for not doing so.

5. Paul was asked to lay down his life for the gospel.

Ridiculous requests lead to ridiculous faith and miraculous promises. Listen to the promise in verse 14: "Thus says the LORD God of Israel: 'The bin of flour shall not be used up, nor shall the jar of oil run dry, until the day the LORD sends rain on the earth'" (1 Kings 17:14).

Quite literally the prophet is saying to this destitute widow, "If you will obey my ridiculous request, you will have food for you and your son for as long as the drought persists." What a deal, right? But she had to give half of what she had to the man of God, trusting God to multiply the meal and oil going forward.

Dee Sapp found herself in a similar position, having to make decisions that would affect her life and future. She had lived an amazing life. The daughter of a pastor, she and her husband, Gary, spent their adult lives in ministry, including more than twenty years as youth directors for a Christian denomination in Louisiana. They pastored and ministered through nonprofit organizations such as Mission of Mercy's One Child Matters program in Colorado, where they worked with children from sixteen third-world countries. The couple has been married nearly fifty years and have two daughters, two sons-in-law, and four grandchildren.

Through years of prayer and seeking God, Gary and Dee learned to hear God's voice and obey. That relationship paid rich dividends in November 1995.

Gary and Dee were preparing to lead fifty-five teens and young adults on a weeklong missions trip to Honduras. For many on the trip this would be a first trip out of the United States. They would see the "mission field" up close and personal. Working with the local missionary, the team would help repair a church building and landscape the grounds. After a hard day's work, they would minister in a church service each evening. Everything was coming together nicely. Gary had spent months organizing, recruiting, and raising funds for the trip. Dee had pulled together household and medical supplies to take along.

Then, two weeks before the departure date, Dee received a surprise announcement from Gary. "He came home and told me he had canceled our flights. We were not going to Honduras! He said the Holy Spirit had spoken to him that we were not to go. Our teenage daughter, Renee, would be the only member of the Sapp family going to Honduras that year."

There was no discussion, no consultation. The deed was done. "I was not happy!" Dee remembers. "I loved working with our missionaries, the Bardwells, and was looking forward to spending 'girl time' with Karen Bardwell. My heart was set on making the trip. I asked Gary why he had decided this and was so sure about it, and he told me the Holy Spirit had not told him the 'why,' but he knew we were not to go! How does one argue against that? I was disappointed, even a bit angry since I had put in so many hours getting things ready. I had to accept the fact that God was looking out for us."

At the time Dee did not realize the connection between the canceled trip and the pain she had been feeling in her abdomen. The pain had come in bouts, on and off, for months. She would feel full and miserable even when she had not eaten. Her stomach would swell, and then it would go back down. The pain would ease, then return full force a few weeks later.

So instead of flying south out of New Orleans to Honduras as originally scheduled, Dee was home when intense abdominal pains hit her the week before Thanksgiving. "The pain was pretty consistent for seven days," she says. "I began to swell; I couldn't eat. Pain would come and go. My plumbing wasn't working too well, and I was so swollen that I looked nine months pregnant."

Her general practitioner, Dr. Buck, believed the culprit was irritable bowel disease and scheduled Dee for extensive tests on Monday, November 27. She never made it to the hospital for those tests. Saturday, November 25, proved to be a critical day. Home alone, hurting, and praying for wisdom, she called her doctor's office for help. Dr. Buck was out for a long Thanksgiving holiday, but the doctor on call listened as Dee described her pain, noted Dr. Buck's previous orders, and prescribed a bowel flush to relieve what appeared to be a blockage.

Dee drove in pain to the nearest pharmacy and picked up the cleansing product. At home she tried to administer it alone. The pain was too great. The Holy Spirit spoke to Dee: "Do not purge yourself or you will surely die." Later Dee's surgeon said purging would likely have caused her death right there in her home.

Dee continued to endure severe pain throughout that Saturday, and focused on praying for the safe return of her daughter and the mission team later that afternoon. When Renee and the mission team arrived at Dee's house and saw her swollen body and the great pain she was in, they laid hands on Dee and prayed.

"This was another life-saving measure," she says. "Prayer changes things. The faith in the hearts of those young people who had just returned from missions work was high."

TRUSTING IN GOD

An hour or so later Dee asked her husband to take her to the emergency room. As he drove, the Holy Spirit instructed Gary to call a friend, Dr. David Remedios, who was a surgeon. The doctor's office reported him out of town for the holidays, but Gary reached him at his home. He agreed to meet Dee and Gary in the emergency center at Rapides Regional Medical Center.

Dee slipped in and out of consciousness on the drive to the hospital. When attendants saw her swollen condition and the pain she was in, Dee was taken immediately to the labor and delivery floor. Nurses thought she was having a baby! Gary answered some unexpected questions before they realized their mistake and returned her to the emergency room.

Dr. Remedios gave Dee a heavy dose of pain medication so she would not suffer. She does not remember what happened Saturday night or the CAT scan performed early Sunday morning. The scan showed Dee's abdominal area to be black and a blockage thought to be in her stomach. Her life depended on finding and removing the cause of the blockage while keeping body poisons confined.

"My surgeon said that if he didn't operate, I would certainly die, yet if he did operate, I would likely die on the operating table or have a major battle for life," she says.

Dr. Remedios said Dee was "the living dead." Performing the surgery was like opening a keg of dynamite and hoping it would not explode. He told Gary there were so many poisons in his wife's body that they could not be cleaned out in time for the surgery.

"We didn't understand what we faced going in," Dee says, "but we placed our trust in God. Just before surgery that Sunday morning, while I was sedated, Dr. Remedios and my husband prayed over me."

Dr. Remedios asked that the Lord would send His angels to guard Dee's life and guide him through the exploratory procedure. During an operation that lasted more than nine hours, he found a diseased gallbladder and appendix, which he removed. He continued to search the stomach, which the CAT scan said contained a blockage. He found none.

Where could it be? Why was a CAT scan, a "picture" of Dee's inner organs, so clearly wrong? Dr. Remedios prayed that God would direct him to the source of the blockage.

God led him into the colon, which he processed with his fingers. There he found a golf-ball-sized cancerous tumor. The cancer had infected her lymph nodes and the intestinal wall. Gangrene had already set in.

Against all medical convention, Dr. Remedios removed three feet of diseased colon, which guaranteed that, if she survived, Dee would wear a colostomy bag for the remainder of her life. But this believing doctor heard heavenly instructions: stretch and reconnect the remaining three feet of colon, and it would work without a bag.

The move was so unconventional that even the assistant surgeon questioned it. Was there enough colon to process waste for normal bowel function? Would the colon hold together? A wrong decision could have cost Dee's life and Dr. Remedios's medical license.

Why take the risk? Dr. Remedios said the Holy Spirit told him not to do the colostomy/ileostomy, as it would hinder Dee in the work He had for her to do. The Holy Spirit told him to stretch the colon, clamp it, attach it, and it would work. Within two days it was functioning perfectly.

"My surgery was a marvel," Dee says now. "I didn't know about the prayer Dr. Remedios and Gary had prayed before surgery began, asking for the angels of the Lord to guard me, but during the time the doctor worked inside my body, I had an angelic visit! I seemed to be looking down on my open body and saw angels at work. I felt as though I was being baptized in a pool of love, and in that instant the fear of death was completely gone. I knew I had a choice to make! I could go on to heaven, or I could let the angels do their work.

"I must tell you, I was drawn to heaven; going there was quite appealing. But I was concerned about the care of my daughter, who was still living at home at the time. I chose to let the angels work."

There were angels inside her body acting "like children," Dee says. "They laughed, rolled, and tumbled as though they were on a trampoline. I believe the angels represented the hand of God guiding Dr. Remedios's fingers as he searched my colon."

Dee remembers that the angels ministered to her during the most dangerous moments of her life. "The warmth and love the angels gave me was astounding," she recalls even today. "Their message to me was, 'Be at peace; all is well.' The angels left and I was alive. I felt great and began to recover at a rapid pace."

God's instructions made the difference. Two days after surgery Dee's bowel function returned. On the third day an oncologist told her she had four months to live without chemotherapy and perhaps a year if she underwent chemo for a year. Were she to survive past a year, the odds were less than 40 percent that she would be alive in five years.

"Mrs. Sapp," the oncologist said, "you are not dealing with reality if you do not do chemo. You need to consider your teenage daughter and husband and do the chemo."

She was surprised to hear Dr. Remedios, a praying Christian, confirm the prognosis.

"So what should I do about taking the chemo?" Dee asked.

"Dee," the good doctor said, "the same Holy Spirit who kept you off the plane to Honduras, who kept you from purging yourself on Saturday, who kept you alive in surgery and gave me instruction on where to look and how to resection your colon is the same Holy Spirit who will tell you what to do about chemo."

Dee was not afraid at the word *cancer* or the diagnosis of four months to live. Angels had visited her; she had been given the choice of life or heaven, and she had chosen life. She knew she was on earth for a reason. The peace of God stayed with her throughout the decision-making process.

"I had no fear whatsoever," she recalls. "I thought it ridiculous to even consider having chemo, much less a year of chemo as the doctor suggested. When the doctor talked about the side effects and the possibility of losing my hair, I told him I had always liked the pixie look, and with my hair as big as Texas, that might be cool! It was my attempt at a joke. I had no intention of doing chemo and would have had none of that if the Lord had not told me specifically to agree."

When Gary and his dad, Leonard, met with the doctor for the post-operation report, they were shocked by what they heard. The diagnosis was stage 3 colon cancer. But very quickly the Holy Spirit brought to Gary's mind the sermon he had preached just a few weeks earlier, "If You Are Always Looking at Your Problem, You'll Never See the Possibility of Your Miracle." Gary chose to declare the possibility of a miracle at that point, and he never wavered. He spoke of it aloud in the hospital, and his family stood with him.

Joined by their pastor, they agreed by faith to believe the report of the Lord, not what was shown in surgery. "My precious mother, though fighting for her own life, pointed her finger at me and declared that I would not die, but would live, because as a child, God had placed Africa on my heart and impressed me that I would go there."

"Mom said, 'Dee, your feet haven't touched African soil yet, and God is not through with you.' She was declaring my future. My first trip to Africa was in 2005, and I've been back three times since.

"I had expected to remain in the hospital for four weeks or more, but I had strength, energy, and peace. I felt well! I had never had major surgery before, so I had no idea that what I was experiencing was not typical."

The day after surgery Dee felt her energy return. Her "plumbing function" returned the second day. Her vital signs were in the right range, and her pain level was mild. She was able to sit in a chair for up to eight hours that first day. All her tubes came out early; she did not need a drain tube from the incision. A miracle was in progress!

God gave Dee a vision in the hospital. He showed her a billboard with the words of Deuteronomy 30:19 written on it: "I call heaven and earth as witnesses today against you, that I have set before you life and death, blessing and cursing; therefore choose life that both you and your descendants may live."

Four days after surgery Dee was released to go home. "God not only healed me of stage 3 colon cancer," she says, "but He gave me a promise for my children." That's when God told her to take the year of chemotherapy, which she did with no negative side effects.

"If Dr. Remedios had not prayed with me about taking chemo," she says, "I don't think I would have kept the appointment. I would have missed God's direction and plan for me.

"I wanted no part of the chemo," she explains, "but God's plan was better. He sent me to a place of darkness to bring me into His light. There is little hope or promise of a good life during most chemo treatments, but God kept me as He promised. I had no negative side effects. Dr. Mansour, my oncologist, kept telling me I was not normal. God's work in me was amazing.

"And people gave me looks of disbelief during chemo. They seemed to ask why, if I was healed, would I take chemo? It was always a joy to tell them the story of how God instructed me to take the treatments."

God turned Dee's obedience into a blessing. "It was amazing to share with patients and families the hope of Christ as Savior and healer at the chemo center."

THE WONDERS OF GOD

A year after the treatment, in December 1996, Dee returned for a colonoscopy to determine if any cancer remained. Dr. Remedios found no lesions, tumors, or cancer—but found a full six feet of healthy, functioning colon! God had performed a creative miracle! That was seventeen years ago.

"My shout out to God is found in Psalm 66:5: 'Take a good look at God's wonders—they'll take your breath away' (THE MESSAGE)."

The experience has made Dee more compassionate, she says. "It has made me look for opportunities to make a difference for others, whether that be a smile, a word, a prayer, or a hug.

"We all have a purpose for being here. We must be busy about our Father's business. I want people to know that God can do anything, even create things, just as His Word tells us."

She says that God was certainly with her every step of the way. "Just imagine," she says, "had the Holy Spirit not spoken to my husband, I would have been on an airplane where the change in pressure would have ruptured my stomach and intestines, and I probably would have died. I'd say God is very interested in me!"

Seventeen years later Dee continues to help her husband in the mission work God has called them to. She travels and gives her testimony wherever the door is open. She has lived a normal, healthy, cancer-free life. Dee had to walk through some ridiculous territory so she could receive the miraculous.

What ridiculous thing is God saying to you today? One would think the widow in 1 Kings 17 would tell the man of God to get lost. He appeared to be another greedy preacher looking for a handout. She did nothing of the sort.

The Bible says "she went away and did according to the word of Elijah" (v. 15). This lady never questioned the words of the prophet. She took what seemed to be a ridiculous action. Ridiculous actions lead to ridiculous faith. Ridiculous faith places us in position to receive the miraculous.

Hebrews 11 provides us the following information concerning people who took ridiculous action and received the miraculous:

1. By faith the elders obtained a good report.

2. By faith Abel offered a better sacrifice than Cain.

3. By faith Enoch escaped death.

4. By faith Noah built an ark and saved his family as well as the human race.

5. By faith Abraham offered Isaac on the altar of sacrifice.

6. By faith Isaac passed the blessing of Abraham to Jacob and Esau.

7. By faith Jacob passed the blessing of Abraham to the sons of Joseph.

8. By faith Joseph looked for a country beyond Egypt.

9. By faith Moses led the children of Israel out of Egypt.

10. By faith Rahab saved the spies and became an ancestor of Christ.

If we need a ridiculous blessing, we may be called upon to take a ridiculous action! Consider the words of 1 Kings 17:15–16: "She went away and did according to the word of Elijah; and she and he and her household ate for many days. The bin of flour was not used up, nor did the jar of oil run dry, according to the word of the LORD which He spoke by Elijah."

We are not told exactly how much time went by between the time this widow made a cake for the man of God, believing she and her son would be taken care of, and the day the Lord sent rain upon the land. The Bible just says she and he and her son did eat many days. What we are sure of is that the drought lasted three and a half years. It is possible the meal and oil lasted for a thousand days or more! The oil and meal did not grow; it just stayed. Every time the widow needed to make a meal, the same amount of flour and oil was there. God's commitment to His people is to supply our every need. If we need it, He has it. If He has it, we can access it.

Sometimes God does not choose to allow us to see the reserves; He asks us to trust Him, believing there will be more than enough. When we step out in obedient faith to do the ridiculous, God has obligated Himself to do the miraculous!

Those who need the miraculous may be called upon to set the miracle in motion by doing the ridiculous. When this lady stepped out in obedient faith, doing the ridiculous, she set in motion the miraculous for both her and her family!

We must also remember that today's miracle is preparing us for the faith needed tomorrow. The widow was no doubt elated that

God had provided the miracle of the meal and oil for so many days, but what she could not have known was that this miracle was preparing her to believe God and the prophet for something on a much larger scale.

The miracle Dee Sapp received in her body was preparation for using the experience to minister to countless people across the world, helping them to believe for a miracle of their own. A miracle is never about one person or one instance; there is always a much greater purpose than the obvious.

At a later time the widow found herself in a predicament. Her son became sick and died. What did she do? She called on the man of God—who raised him to life! There is no doubt God's daily provision of the meal and oil figured into her faith to believe her son would experience a resurrection. If this woman had not trusted the man of God in the little things, she could never have trusted him for her son!

What Elijah's widow and Dee's husband, Gary, have in common is a propensity to believe the voice of God. The widow gave her last meal away, and Gary canceled a mission trip. The decision of the widow saved her family; Gary's decision saved Dee's life.

What is God preparing you for? Are you going to pass or fail the present test? If you pass this test, you will be placing yourself and your family in the pathway of a blessing at a more crucial time. If you need the miraculous, you must be willing to do the ridiculous! If you need God to do something ridiculous in your life, please pray this prayer with me:

> *Dear Lord Jesus, I stand in need of a miracle. I am totally incapable of supplying my own need. I cast myself upon Your mercy today, knowing You are a merciful God. I believe that what You did for the widow and Dee Sapp, You stand ready to do for me. I commit myself to*

do whatever You ask of me, no matter how ridiculous it may seem. When my obedience has been fulfilled, I am expecting to see the miraculous in my life. I call my miracle forth from the presence of God today. I receive the miracle that I need and call it done in the name of Jesus. Amen.

Ten

DO YOU WANT A BABY?

ONE OF THE great stories in the Word of God is set in the Old Testament book of 1 Samuel and has to do with a woman named Hannah, who could not conceive or bear children. In that era the inability to have children was considered a curse from God.

Each of us has experienced circumstances that have overshadowed or colored the good that happens to us. This was precisely Hannah's situation. Her husband loved her; in fact, the Bible says he favored her above everyone else to the point that he provided her with twice as much as he gave others. Her husband had come to terms with Hannah's barrenness; the sorrow and shame of childlessness seemed to be Hannah's to bear alone. Every good thing that transpired for Hannah was downgraded because she could not have children. Nothing but a child could satisfy her. Consequently Hannah moved from a hopeless victim of circumstance to a bold woman who was proactive in audacious prayer.

The prayer of Hannah was emotional. She did not pray out loud in the worship place, but her lips gave evidence of her intense petition to God. To Eli, the high priest, she appeared drunk, and he confronted her.

Listen to the words of Hannah. "No, my lord, I am a woman of sorrowful spirit. I have drunk neither wine nor intoxicating drink, but have poured out my soul before the LORD. Do not consider your maidservant a wicked woman, for out of the abundance of my complaint and grief I have spoken until now" (1 Sam. 1:15–16). The audacity of her prayers gained her the favor she needed to bring her situation to an acceptable conclusion.

Hannah's story is much like that of Mike and Amanda Wilson of Houston, Texas. Mike and Amanda met in church when they were teenagers. Eleven years later they exchanged vows at a beautiful Southern plantation home near Houston. It was a fairy tale come to life.

"Like most couples, we had a five-year plan," Amanda says today. But a year and a half into the marriage, she and Mike knew they were on a faster track. They wanted children and began taking steps to start their family. Amanda stopped using birth control, they became earnest about saving money, and they converted the guest bedroom into a nursery. Over the weeks she and Mike sold off unneeded furniture to provide funds for nursery "paraphernalia." The couple would curl up on the sofa for long talks about how a baby would change their lives, how their priorities would shift, and what they wanted in schools and friends for their children. As the months went by, they made conceiving a top priority.

According to their "perfect plan," pregnancy would happen easily once they decided they were ready. It never crossed their minds they might have problems conceiving. "I don't think I can say that I really knew how important having children was to us then," Amanda says. "It was the trials we went through that made us realize what a true gift it is to conceive and carry a life to full term."

Having children was a desire that grew deeper and stronger as time went by. Mike and Amanda knew they wanted to be parents, but it wasn't until it seemed that parenting wasn't a viable option that they knew their desire was a genuine need for them.

"As we realized initially my body was contributing to the problem,

I dealt with the guilt," she explains. "I felt I was keeping Mike from becoming a father. I knew what an amazing dad he would be and felt I was failing at something that I, as a woman, was supposed to be able to do."

Unsuccessful attempts to conceive seemed to make the weeks and months stand still. "Every single day consisted of testing, praying, hoping, and waiting. Those were the longest days of my life," she acknowledges.

After six months of trying, Amanda stopped having monthly cycles. This seemed to be a very encouraging sign to the couple, but a trip to the doctor revealed she wasn't ovulating. The fact that she was not ovulating made becoming pregnant impossible, and their hope fell.

At age eighteen Amanda had a grapefruit-size tumor removed from her ovary. The doctor now explained that the removal had left her with only a partial ovary, which contributed to her difficulty getting pregnant. As a result, the doctor put her on Clomid, a drug that stimulates an increase in the amount of hormones that support ovulation, and increased the dosage over a few months. She went through the same thing with metformin.

Amanda started and stopped various birth control pills to try to jump-start her monthly cycles, but these efforts proved futile. She also tried ovulation predictors, but all her efforts were in vain.

After a year of frustration they changed doctors. "We were still believing that God was going to make us parents," Amanda says. "The hardest part, as any woman who has gone through fertility issues can attest, is that during this process, it seemed like everyone else was getting pregnant—even women who never wanted to be pregnant!" Amanda was a high school theater director; to her dismay, sixteen-year-old girls were having unwanted babies in high school while she and her husband could not conceive though they desperately wanted to do so.

"It was almost unbearable to have a deep desire to be a parent, to experience pregnancy, to have a child to invest in and raise and not to be able to do the simplest thing: get pregnant." Their desires seemed reasonable enough; they just wanted a child to love. Mike and Amanda found it very hard to understand how their greatest desire could be the wrong path for them. Amanda stated what most women in her situation have wrestled with: "I couldn't wrap my head around why God would build such a strong desire in me to be a mom then not allow that desire to be fulfilled."

The same thing happened to Hannah. She had an insatiable desire to have children but was powerless to conceive. Sometimes it is very difficult to understand how the path we are on is in any way just, or of all things, the will of God for us. We must never forget, "The steps of a good man are ordered by the LORD" (Ps. 37:23). We may not always understand where we are in life, but in difficult times we can trust and believe that a miracle is just over the horizon. Remember, God knows what we do not know, sees what we cannot see, and works in ways that we cannot fathom.

As it did for Hannah of old, Mike and Amanda concede, "The wait took its toll." Amanda found it increasingly difficult to remain positive and patient. "We continued to pray and dedicate ourselves to God, asking Him to use the time to form us into who we needed to be as spouses for each other. We asked God to equip us to handle whatever specific things our kids would go through in life and to give us wisdom before those things ever came along."

WAITING PATIENTLY

Interestingly Mike and Amanda found themselves praying that God would remind them of His patience so they might extend the same grace to their future children. They prayed this prayer as they waited patiently to see if they were, in fact, expecting a child.

After a second year Amanda began to withdraw. She grew weary of discussing the ordeal with even her best friends. There was no excitement or hope left in recounting the story.

"I reached a place where the only person I could talk to about the ordeal was my mom," she remembers. "I told her about the fertility steps we were taking and how nothing was working. Many nights I would sit up until late in the night talking to her on the phone, most of the time talking through my tears."

Scripture says Hannah became so distraught that "she was in bitterness of soul, and…wept in anguish" (1 Sam. 1:10). What a descriptive verse! Hannah was tormented by her inability to give birth to a child, and Amanda found herself in the very same situation. The sorrow of the empty arms of a woman who wants to be a mother is unequaled.

Consider the words of Rachel in Genesis 30:1: "When Rachel saw that she bore Jacob no children, Rachel envied her sister, and said to Jacob, 'Give me children, or else I die!'"

One of Mike and Amanda's new doctors did blood work and ultrasounds to check hormone levels, which proved normal. The doctor was unable to identify exactly why she wasn't ovulating, especially after the rounds of initial medications she had taken. Ultrasounds revealed polycystic ovary syndrome, which meant Amanda's body had eggs, but these were not reaching a viable size to initiate the ovulation process. Instead of ovulating one egg each month, as most women do, Amanda was ovulating many eggs. Amanda remembers, "I had a lot of eggs too small to impregnate. They just sat in my ovaries, never traveling, thus never creating an opportunity for fertilization."

Time and again a new procedure awakened hope in this young couple, but it was soon met by the disappointing news that once again Amanda was not pregnant. One hopeful season included a daily morning injection of the drugs Follistim, Menopur, and Ovidrel in addition to blood work and an ultrasound every other morning. All this had to be done before heading to the high school to fulfill her teaching duties.

"I was pumped full of hormones and in an already heightened emotional situation. I believed this would lead to a baby in short order."

It did not!

One of the peripheral pressures this couple faced was the weight of finances. Each procedure cost money—lots of money—and their insurance company would pay for only two rounds of treatments and two attempts at artificial insemination. Amanda knew, "If we did not conceive after those two rounds, we were on our own financially. We both knew we could not afford to do this alone."

Even with insurance the drug regimen was nearly cost-prohibitive. "I remember getting a phone call at work explaining exactly what I was going to have to do and how much it would cost. I just broke down and wept. I was overwhelmed. I left work that day because I couldn't pull myself together."

Another problem with the plan was that in vitro fertilization was not covered at all. That procedure alone was more than ten thousand dollars.

From a physical and financial perspective it appeared that the hope of parenthood was well out of their reach. We must never forget that when things are out of reach for us, they are very accessible to the God we serve. The real challenge we face in times like this is whether we can maintain a positive attitude and a heart full of faith despite the odds.

To have a child, Mike and Amanda took every option available to them: daily injections, blood work, and ultrasounds. Amanda explains, "Because my body had so many eggs, each one had to be measured to make sure it wasn't being overstimulated. I needed a certain number of eggs at certain sizes for the doctor to feel comfortable with the insemination."

After preparing financially for in vitro fertilization, Mike and Amanda were finally ready for her first insemination. "We were so excited," Amanda says. "I just knew God was going to honor our patience and desire." She followed the doctor's instructions to a T. She took two days off work and lay in bed without moving, praying that the fertilization would be successful. Mike stayed with her, waiting on her hand and foot, and offering support.

Amanda remembers, "Mike did everything he could possibly do, but at a certain point, a man cannot understand what a woman feels when she aches to be a mother. My pain and disappointment was not something he could comprehend."

For two long weeks they awaited anxiously for what was supposed to usher in the glad news of pregnancy. On Friday Amanda went for blood work to see if the hormone levels in her blood had increased, an indication of a viable pregnancy. Over the weekend, as she waited for the results of her blood work, she started her cycle—for the first time in more than a year! Amanda was devastated.

"I was in disbelief," she recalls. "This could not be happening. I knew that I was going to be—that I was meant to be—a mother. We had planned out the theme for the nursery; I had ordered art for the room in faith that a baby would come." All she could do was hope that somehow the evidence of that horrible weekend would be a mistake, that the blood work from the doctor's office would reveal a pregnancy.

Amanda recalls, "I called the doctor's office crying, and they sympathetically confirmed that my blood work showed I was not pregnant. The next day I opened our mail to find the artwork I had ordered for the nursery. It was like an upending blow."

Sometimes God sends little reminders of His faithfulness, like the arrival of the artwork, to let us know that He really does intend to work things out for us. When we are in the middle of the predicament, it is easy to mistake the little signs of God's care for a devastating reminder of the ongoing dilemma.

Not surprisingly, Amanda sank into a deep depression. She was unwilling to speak to anyone, and she cried through the day. Her thoughts were only about having a child, holding a child.

"I begged and yelled at God. He was clearly being cruel. Why did I want this so badly; why was God putting us through this financial and emotional drain only to be left wanting? I stopped talking to my friends. I spent my lunch hour in my car crying out in despair. My entire being was consumed with this need. I didn't have the energy or desire to focus on anything else, and all I had to show for it was heartache."

She let her body recover for a few months and then started the process all over again—only this time she did so with much less hope than before. Then the hammer fell again. The doctor confirmed that Mike had a very low sperm count. With her inability to ovulate and his inability to produce sperm, the doctor said the couple would never conceive outside the help of modern medicine. Mike and Amanda felt that God and modern medicine had failed them.

The turning point came in an unexpected time and place. Of all days, it was Mother's Day, the most painful of all holidays for Amanda. She and Mike sat in their usual place at our church, Christian Temple Church in Houston, as my wife, Susan Nordin, brought the morning message. It was a stirring account of one of the covenants mentioned in the Old Testament. Her sermon title was, "Throw Your Shoe at It."

The sermon was based on the Old Testament shoe covenant that was designed to affirm an agreement between contractual parties. Susan's sermon declared that passing a shoe from one participant in an agreement to another symbolized the transference of ownership. Giving a shoe to someone confirmed that the deal had been signed, sealed, and delivered. The last act of the shoe covenant was that each participant would throw the shoe over the head of the other participants as they rehearsed the conditions of the covenant. (See Ruth 4:7–12.)

"I listened and applied that message to Mike and me," Amanda said. "I realized the significance of what was being said. I understood that I had been holding on to my own plans and dreams when I needed to put my trust in God."

Amanda had spent months refusing to let anyone in, refusing to let go of her plans while attempting to retain control over everything pertaining to a possible pregnancy.

She remembers, "In that moment I knew what had to happen. Without saying a word, Mike and I joined hands and walked down for prayer. I remember the genuine catharsis of that altar time. We stood together and wept, and for the first time in a long time shared the experience with each other. The Lord ministered to both of us, uniting us and restoring our hope. By the time we reached the car to go home, we knew there was an urgent action that needed to occur."

Despite feeling awkward about taking such an unusual step of faith, Amanda and Mike stood in the doorway of the room they had prepared as a baby's nursery and did exactly what the speaker had described. Because they were both part of the problem, they decided each should have a shoe thrown over them. Amanda says, "We took turns sitting in the doorway of the empty room and threw a shoe over each other. Mike prayed as he threw one over me; I prayed as I threw one over him. In that moment we believed God was going to bring this to pass for us."

The fact that this was happening on Mother's Day made it all the more significant to this young couple. Pastor Susan would later acknowledge that this was the first Mother's Day she had ever deviated from a Mother's Day theme, but she felt the Lord had spoken to her that He wanted to do miracles for multiple families in the church on that day. As a result she decided to challenge the faith of individuals and families in the congregation who had been praying for a miracle without seeing any obvious evidence that it was coming to pass.

Amanda explains that things didn't get easier after that act of faith, only that they knew something had been set in motion. "I didn't cry every day. I didn't get frustrated as easily. Best of all, my husband and I were connecting again, and the Lord was now not just someone we were bringing our petitions to, but the One who was carrying us."

NOW OR NEVER

After the arduous regimen of daily injections and vitamins, it came time for the second and last insemination. Amanda went in for a final ultrasound and blood work.

"I was sitting in my office, getting ready for an after-school theater rehearsal, when the phone rang. The nurse told me that the thing we had been trying to avoid, overstimulation, had in fact happened. They were not going to go through with the insemination."

The nurse apologized and told Amanda the doctor would try again in another month. For Amanda, though, it was now or never. "We couldn't afford to lose this round of treatment. I had been through too much physically, emotionally, and financially to suddenly have that stifled. I was hysterical. My final hopes seemed to be slipping through my fingers. I could see no happy solutions. I felt totally out of control of the situation, then remembered what we had prayed at the altar that Mother's Day. This was no longer my 'property,' or my problem to deal with. We had willingly relinquished control of the situation to the Lord and had promised God that we would trust Him to see us through."

Amanda called the doctor. "We're coming in tomorrow," she said. "We need to proceed and see what will happen."

Overnight they scraped together the ten thousand dollar fee and then went in for the egg retrieval process. Amanda had ovulated twenty-three eggs! The doctor fertilized the ones that survived a trial period of a few days. They waited to see which ones were the strongest of the remaining eggs.

The next week the couple returned for the "egg transfer." They chose to have three embryos transferred into her womb. Again, Amanda followed the doctor's prescribed regimen. Ten days later, she bought a bulk pack of home pregnancy tests and took the first one. The indication was faint but visible—positive! She kept the news to herself, not even telling Mike. The next day she took a second test, also positive!

"I was sitting in the same place in my office where I had received the bad news about my first insemination when the phone rang," Amanda recalls. "This time the doctor greeted me with the words, 'Hello, Mama!'" Mike and Amanda were overjoyed as they broke the good news to family and friends.

After the initial blood work, they had to return to the doctor's office to make certain her hormone levels were rising appropriately. The phone call came on her birthday, September 17, and the word they received was, "Everything was as it should be." What a great birthday present!

Later that week Mike and Amanda went in for their first ultrasound. Much to their surprise, the doctor said, 'Here's an embryo, and here's another one! Twin A and Twin B!"

Mike and Amanda drove home laughing and rejoicing that they were having two children after throwing two shoes in their shoe-covenant prayer the previous Mother's Day. What could be more perfect!

Caedyn James and Mackenzie Prestin were born at 1:05 and 1:06

in the evening, April 1, 2010. They weighed in at barely more than three pounds. Their faces were about the size of oranges. Because of their small size, the parents were not allowed to hold them for several days. The time passed quickly and served to intensify their desire to hold the twins.

Amanda remembers, "The very next Mother's Day at Christian Temple, Mike and I were back in our usual seat, this time holding our two miracle children. We brought Caedyn and Mackenzie to the altar, where we dedicated them to the Lord. We stood in the same spot where the Lord had brought comfort and help to us one year earlier. Once again we were immersed in His presence."

It would be impossible to put into words the pain this young couple experienced during their years of disappointment, but it is equally impossible to form words that honor God for the joy and healing He brought to their hearts when He established their home with beautiful twins. God is more than faithful.

Mike and Amanda say, "We learned that God cannot be bribed, cajoled, or worn down. An answer to prayer doesn't come to the person who is deserving enough; it comes to the ones who are broken enough, who surrender their all to God. We learned that what we really needed was to give ourselves to God, and when we did that, He gave us everything our hearts desired."

Just as the Lord heard Mike and Amanda's cry for a child, He also heard Hannah's audacious prayer. "Eli answered and said, 'Go in peace, and the God of Israel grant your petition which you have asked of Him'" (1 Sam. 1:17).

Hannah was so sure that Eli had heard from God that from the moment he spoke those prophetic words, her faith never wavered. Remember, Hannah had been seeking God for a child for years, yet upon one word from the man of God she responded in an audacious manner: "The woman went her way and ate, and her face was no longer sad" (v. 18). It is interesting to note that the Bible never makes reference to Hannah praying about this again, but it does reference the fact that she worshipped God. It is a wonderful thing to know that you have heard from God and the answer is on its way!

Mike and Amanda knew from the day they threw the shoes over one another that God was going to give them a miracle. Just like Hannah, their miracle was not immediate, but it was imminent.

> Elkanah knew Hannah his wife, and the LORD remembered her. So it came to pass in the process of time that Hannah conceived and bore a son, and called his name Samuel, saying, "Because I have asked for him from the LORD."
> —1 SAMUEL 1:19–20

What have you asked of God? I want to remind you that God is no more faithful to Hannah or Mike and Amanda than He is going to be to you! There is a time to quit praying and start worshipping, and I believe that time is *now* for you to do just that!

If you have been believing God for something that is yet to come to pass, please pray the following prayer with me:

Dear Lord Jesus, I am believing You for this miracle to come to pass in my life [name the miracle]. I have petitioned You for this in the past, and I am once again asking for Your provision. I believe this to be Your will, and today is the day I begin to stand on Your promise for this miracle. By an act of my own will I am now *going to transition from petition to praise! I thank You for Your faithfulness to Your promises. I worship You in advance of the promise being manifest in the physical because I believe it has already happened in the spiritual realm. Your Word and Your promise are the highest forms of reality, and I choose to believe in what I know Your will*

to be rather than what I see being manifested in my life.
Thank You for the fulfillment of Your promise in my life.
I receive Your miracle, in Jesus's name. Amen.

Eleven

WILL YOU HAVE MERCY ON ME?

*I*N LUKE 17 we find Jesus spending time with His disciples. As He passes through the countryside of Samaria and Galilee, He speaks spiritual truth into them. For some reason His travels take them near a leper colony. Ten lepers rush out to meet Him, an act strictly forbidden under the Law.

Leprosy was a disease for which there was no known cure. It was the most dreaded disease of the day, and those affected by it felt the devastating consequences of such a diagnosis. Once a person was found to have contracted this horrific disease, everything changed in and around their lives.

A leper was not admitted to a hospital and given aggressive treatment; he was banished to a leper colony. A leper colony was one of the crudest, most disgusting places imaginable. This disease had affected everyone within the colony. Some had been recently diagnosed; others were languishing in its final throes. Some had lost the extremities of their bodies; for others, the disease was almost undetectable. Whatever their situations, all who found themselves in the colony were awaiting the curtain call of their lives.

One cannot imagine the hopelessness these lepers must have felt in such a place. Hopelessness affects everything. As long as we have hope, the possibility of a comeback exists. When we lose hope, our chances of a recovery, from whatever condition, are slim to none.

The Bible says, "We have this hope as an anchor for the soul, firm and secure. It enters the inner sanctuary behind the curtain" (Heb. 6:19, NIV). As we know, the soul is our mind, will, and emotions. If hope is the anchor of the soul, then the thing that anchors our mind, will, and emotions is hope in God and hope for the future. Hope is tied to faith; it is impossible to have faith when hope has been lost. When one has taken two jars of sand and poured them into one larger jar, it becomes impossible to separate them again. In the same way, faith and hope are inextricably intermingled.

If we had visited that leper colony with Jesus and His disciples, the most striking thing we would have seen would not have been the physical condition of the residents but the hopelessness that stared out through empty eyes from the "prisoners" in the camp. When a person was declared infected with this dreaded disease, the priest banished him to the leper colony. For all practical purposes the declaration was a life sentence. A leper was to leave his home and family immediately and live with others who shared his sentence. I cannot imagine the sorrow of a trip to the leper colony. I am sure most arrived with tears coursing down their cheeks because of the despair they felt. Perhaps some never arrived, dying instead of a broken heart during the journey.

I am sure the first few weeks in the colony held the loneliest days a leper would ever experience as the reality of his condition and future settled upon him. At first, perhaps, a leper thought he would wake up the next morning to find he was at home with his family once again.

Such is the case with most people who receive a diagnosis of a terminal disease from a doctor: "Surely this is not true, is it? Perhaps there is some mistake? Should I get a second opinion?" Then the reality of the prognosis settles in and the loss of hope begins to erode faith. A plummeting faith level begins to deplete hope, and one becomes trapped in a downward spiral out of which some never emerge.

It is apparent that word of Jesus's recent miracles had found its way into the leper colony. Read the words penned in Luke 17:12–13: "And as he entered a certain village, there met Him ten men that were lepers, which stood afar off. And they lifted up their voices and said, Jesus, Master, have mercy on us!" (KJV). These lepers "stood afar off" because the Law demanded that lepers have absolutely no physical contact with an unaffected individual; they were considered highly contagious and ceremonially unclean.

Because these individuals were unclean, they could have no further physical contact with anyone, including a husband or wife, a mother or child, a grandparent or grandchild—a devastating reality. Not only did they realize their condition was terminal, but they were also painfully aware that life as they knew it was over. Their situation would get measurably worse until the end.

Such was the condition of the ten lepers who cried out to Jesus. "They lifted up their voices, and said, Jesus, Master, have mercy on us." Jesus was their only remaining hope. Even though they could not have physical contact with Jesus, they were not about to let their last hope for a miracle slip away.

Wanda Cook knows what it's like when doctors say all hope is gone. Her story, shared in her own words, is proof that doctors never have the final say.

∾

A RECURRING DREAM

Our youngest son, Austin, was born in 2001, the same year terrorists attacked the World Trade Center in New York City. I grieved as did the rest of the country, but by 2006 I began seeing that terrible event in a new way.

Early that year I began to have horrible dreams about those attacks. I had the same dream every night for months. I saw myself standing in the rubble, the smell of death all around, and bricks and glass crashing around me. I experienced the tragedy as if I were standing within it, surrounded by it, awake and alive. I smelled the fire and death. I heard the screams and felt the terror as if it were my own.

I shared my dreams with my husband, Destin, but neither of us could understand why I was experiencing this. The event had happened five years earlier, yet for some reason God was using it to draw me closer to Him. Through these dreams He gave me an insatiable hunger for His Word; I couldn't get enough of the Scriptures. I found myself making my way to the church every day, lying on my face at the altar and crying for hours on end. I began to wonder if I was losing my mind. Looking back now, I know God was working, preparing me for the battle that would soon hit us.

Destin and I decided to take Tyler, our oldest, and Austin and get away on our first all-family vacation. We went to the beach, a place we had always felt closest to God. The sound of crashing waves seemed to wash away the cares of the world. Finally together as a family, we found ourselves caught up with the beauty of the oceanfront, and we enjoyed a relaxing, happy week with the boys. Nothing could be more relaxing or refreshing than spending a week on the beach as a family.

We had a really terrific time. Our sole concern was that Austin, who had always loved to be in the water, had no desire to be outside. He refused to play; he wanted only to remain inside and lie around. Destin and I decided that as soon as we returned home, we would take him to the pediatrician for a checkup. After all, we had noticed a bump on his head; it had been there for a while, but we had thought nothing of it. A bump on the head of a five-year-old boy is pretty typical. When he had said it did not hurt, we forgot about it.

After a week we reluctantly said good-bye to the beach. No one wanted to leave; even Austin, who had not gone near the water, did not want to go back home. Perhaps he sensed our lives would never be the same.

A week later, in June 2006, I sat in the pediatrician's office, reading reports alone before the doctor came to answer my myriad of questions. I was reeling from what I was seeing. All I could think to ask was, "Is this as serious as I think it is?"

"More serious than you can realize right now," the doctor answered. "In fact, I have you set up with a neurologist in Pittsburgh first thing tomorrow morning. You need to get started; Austin can't wait." When the pediatrician made it a point to emphasize that Austin should be taken to Pittsburg the next day, I paid close attention.

It was there in the pediatrician's office that memories of the recurring dreams began surging over me like waves of the ocean over a person lost at sea. That vision—those smells, those screams—flooded my senses at that moment, just as they had for so many months before. I realized those dreams were intended to prepare me for what was to come next. They were a warning from the Lord that we were going to confront the greatest challenge of our lives, but God would see us through. We would not only survive, but we would also thrive.

It was confirmed the next day that my five-year-old son had cancer, though the doctors needed four additional weeks after the initial biopsy to determine the type. Those four ensuing weeks were extremely difficult as we waited to hear what Austin's prognosis and treatment would be.

Eventually Austin was diagnosed with stage 4 clear cell carcinoma. The primary tumor, about the size of a Nerf football, had consumed his right kidney and had metastasized to his head. He had two nodules on one of his lungs. To confirm the diagnosis, our doctor wanted to remove the primary tumor and have it evaluated. Distraught but believing, we gave our son over to surgery.

As anyone with knowledge of medical science knows, four tumors in three different locations within one body are a foreboding sign. We were absolutely demoralized. It is very easy to lose hope in such a situation. All kinds of questions, images, and fears tried to rip away all the faith we held to.

Surgery brought witness to our first God-sized miracle. The cancer had in fact metastasized yet could not be found in any of the glands around the kidney. This was nothing short of a miracle! The news gave us a ray of hope. We clung to it like a drowning man to a life preserver.

To help us understand the magnitude of Austin's challenge, Destin and I were told that only nine children had been diagnosed with this kind of cancer in the past five years. Only nine in five years! His was a very rare condition, and the problem with very rare conditions is that very little is known about how to treat them. The seriousness of this information was not lost on us.

Our oncologist sought out the doctors who had treated the previous nine patients, and together they drew up a treatment plan. None of them would give us a prognosis or personal opinion about how they believed the plan would play out. I must say, the fact that the medical team had little confidence in their collective judgment was very disconcerting. It would have been very easy to give up hope right then, except that God had prepared us for this battle months before. Now His Word sustained us.

No one would consider removing the tumor from Austin's head until it could be reduced in size because surgery was too dangerous. Destin and I sought the

Lord and reminded Him of the Word He had been storing up in us for months now. Because He had prepared us in advance, we decided to wage war on the devil and the cancer in Austin's body.

Partnering with family, friends, and churches across the nation, we embarked on a year of intense prayer, believing God for a miracle. The tumor remained in Austin's head during the onset of treatment. Through chemo, radiation, numerous surgeries, and blood transfusions, God never left our side.

The side effects of chemotherapy ravaged Austin's body. We watched as his body deteriorated and began to reject some of the medicines. The effects of the disease and treatments took a huge toll on his young body. It was a very difficult process to walk through with him.

We prayed for wisdom as to whether we should continue with treatment. We had reached a point where we were discussing what quality of life Austin would have going forward if he survived.

The faith of a child is amazing. Austin became the teacher, and we became his students. We began to see the world through his eyes. He had a simplicity and composure we had never noticed before. Our little boy would talk to us about heaven. He described what he would see when he closed his eyes to sleep. He said angels would visit him. He drew pictures in bright, vivid colors and explained what he had seen the previous night in his dreams. His body looked nearly dead, but his countenance was radiant, like one who had been in the presence of the Almighty. It was amazing how the Lord was with our son. He was there throughout the long nights and days and fulfilled His promise to be "with you always even unto the end of the world" (Matt. 28:20, KJV).

Our year of praying helped me understand the story of Lazarus as never before. Jesus did not rush to Lazarus's side when He got the news that Lazarus was sick; it was not the right time. Believe it or not, He waited until Lazarus was dead before He came, but He showed up with a plan for a turnaround, and we believed for one as well. We don't always understand God's timing.

Because of Jesus's timing in the story of Lazarus, many Jews converted because they witnessed a man being raised from the dead. Jesus was deeply troubled when He saw the crowd crying. He wept! He knows and feels our pain, and we knew for certain He was walking this long, painful road with us!

After months of chemo and radiation, the neurologist decided to perform an MRI to see if the cancer was responding to treatment. The test proved that it was, indeed, responding; we were told the tumor was only in the skull and was, in fact, shrinking. However, they said, the initial diagnosis was wrong. The tumor had penetrated the brain. This was a devastating blow. I cannot begin to explain what a setback this appeared to be.

Our friends decided to form a prayer chain. People committed to pray nonstop for a miracle until we went to surgery. Chemo was discontinued so Austin's body could strengthen.

Then came our second God-sized miracle. When the surgeon went in to remove the tumor, he found it did not have to be cut away from the brain. Not only could he just slice it off the brain, he found living, active bone cells working to repair the area around a tumor that happened to be dead. It was as if the brain was cradling the tumor.

The doctor was astounded. He said, "Chemo doesn't recognize good or bad cells; it attacks them all. For bone to be producing living, active cells that are trying to repair the body is just unheard of."

"Our God specializes in the unheard of!" we quickly replied.

We were blessed with many miracles in that yearlong battle, and many people witnessed them. It was simply amazing to watch Him work when it seemed there was no way out. He is Jehovah Jireh, and He certainly provided for our family.

Along the way we suffered through nights without sleep from fear that Austin was nearing his last breath. We learned then that God could do what we could not do and be where we could not be. We learned to place our son in His hands and believe Him to bring Austin through the troubled water of this terrible disease.

All the while I was aware that if God lifted His hand of protection from me for a moment, I would die from heartache. I cannot describe the pain of a parent watching her child face almost certain death. Our prayer was then, and still is, "God, if we have to go through this fire, be glorified in it and through all we say and do."

We grabbed hold of God's mighty hand as we read, "'For the mountains shall depart and the hills be removed, but My kindness shall not depart from you, nor shall My covenant of peace be removed,' says the LORD, who has mercy on you" (Isa. 54:10). We found great comfort in knowing that though our world was falling apart, His love for us could not be shaken. His peace in our life was unexplainable. Even when the heart hurts, and we won't deny that it does, there is peace in the midst of it all.

Austin in now twelve years old and is flourishing. He is at the top of his class academically and is learning to play the trumpet to the glory of God. Every time I hear him blow his horn, I think of the nodules that were once in his lungs, and I want to shout! His condition is actively followed by doctors every six months to make sure cancer cells have not returned, and his case has been studied all across the nation. Today Austin is cancer free and healthy!

God has also brought to life in us the word of Psalm 66:16: "Come and hear, all you who fear God, and I will declare what He has done for my soul." He birthed a ministry of hope and encouragement, as Destin and I travel the nation telling of the miracles we witnessed during our painful time. We testify that He is the "Prince of Peace."

∽

RIDING OUT THE STORM

Anchoring our faith deep in the knowledge of who He is, then riding out the storm, can only produce real perseverance.

The lepers cried out to Jesus, and He told them, "Go and show yourself to the priest" (Luke 5:14). The only way a person who had been banished to a leper colony could return home to family and jobs was to visit the priest and be pronounced clean. The Bible makes us aware that as they went to show themselves to the priest, they were cleansed from the dreaded disease of leprosy. Sometimes healing is instant and sometimes it is a process; either way, Jesus is the healer.

All ten lepers were cleansed. This was proved by the fact that as Jesus continued on His way, one Samaritan leper returned to give Him thanks. Gratitude is more a decision than a set of circumstances. Some people seem to have it all, yet are not grateful. Others seem to have very little, yet live a grateful life! What is the difference? Gratitude is not an emotion; it is a choice of a lifestyle.

The Samaritan leper fell at the feet of Jesus giving thanks, which proved he had been cleansed; otherwise he could not have come near to Jesus because of the restrictions of his disease. It is here that something very interesting happened. Jesus tells the lone Samaritan leper to get up and go his way because his faith had made him *"whole"* (Luke 17:19, KJV, emphasis added). All ten were cleansed, but only one was made whole! Ten lepers were cured of their leprosy, but I believe the lone Samaritan leper was made whole. Whatever the effects this terminal disease had inflicted upon him were instantly reversed.

I see the lone Samaritan leper watching as fingers and toes reappeared. Nasty scars began to disappear. He was made whole. The God we serve is not relegated to just moving us forward from our station in life. He is capable of making us whole, restoring everything the devil has stolen from us. The lone leper received a creative miracle from Jesus, and so did Austin Cook! Austin's bones began to grow and produce new bone. Only God can do a thing like that, and He is our God. He can do a creative miracle when one is needed.

I do not know what the enemy has stolen from you, but I can tell you that God has very good intentions toward you. If you will turn your condition over to Him, He will make something wonderful of it.

The prophet Jeremiah declared, "For I know the thoughts and plans that I have for you, says the Lord, thoughts and plans for welfare and peace and not for evil, to give you hope in your final outcome" (Jer. 29:11, AMP). The plan of God for the final disposition of your problem is to use it for your good and His glory!

But notice the last phrase of that verse: "to give you hope in your final outcome." Hope was depleted in the leper colony, and it was low in the Cook family at the beginning of Austin's battle, but it was certainly not dead!

I challenge you to fan whatever faith and hope you have left into a full-blown flame because your God is on the scene and on the job. If He is present, you are a candidate for a miracle. So get ready for some good news: He is bringing it to pass.

If you or anyone you know is in need of a miracle, please pray this prayer with me:

Jesus, I cry out to You today, just as did the lepers and the Cook family. I call to You, knowing that what You have done for others You will do for me. The situation I face is beyond my control, but I know it is not beyond Your control. I give it to You today, and I am believing for a good outcome. I give You praise in advance of the appearance of my miracle. You are great, and to You will belong all the glory for this miracle, in Jesus's name. Amen.

Twelve

WILL YOU HEAL MY SON?

THE GREATEST RESPONSIBILITY a human being can be given is to raise a child from infancy to adulthood. Many unforeseen challenges lie in the path. Every parent knows the twists and turns, the heartbreaks and disappointments that raising a child can bring. But there are also too many joys to count. Most of my favorite times in life have to do with raising my two children. My wife and I had an absolute blast during those wonderful years.

As a lead pastor for more than thirty years, I have had the privilege of dedicating hundreds of children to the Lord. I remind the parents, "This is really a parent dedication; we just call it a baby dedication." The truth is that when we dedicate children, we are giving the child back to God for His purpose, but we are committing ourselves to raise that child for God and to lead by example.

Once the child has been committed to the Lord, His expectation is for us to raise *His* child (we gave them back to God so they belong to Him) according to His Word! He also expects us to instill within that child character traits that are in keeping with a godly life. The example we set will have much to do with where that child will spend eternity. As parents we must remember, there is no greater calling on earth than to pour into a child. We get only one chance; we must not be asleep at the wheel.

Part of being a great parent is being fully engaged at every level.

Far too many adults abdicate the responsibility of their children to a day care, school, or church. While there is nothing wrong with those institutions, the weight of accountability for the future and eternity of a child rests squarely on the shoulders of the parents. Fully engaged parents will exhibit genuine concern for the welfare of that child, no matter what is going on.

In Luke 8 we are introduced to a fully engaged father. The chapter actually opens with several women ministering to Jesus. Each of them had received a miracle from Him. Among them was Mary Magdalene, out of whom Jesus had cast seven devils.

The chapter continues with the parable of the sower and the seed, then moves on to the parable of letting our light shine. As Jesus was teaching the multitude, His mother, Mary, and His brothers arrive. Because of the crowd they could not approach Him.

Once He was finished teaching, Jesus and His entourage boarded a ship to cross the sea and found themselves in a great storm that threatened the ship and their lives. Exhausted from the activities of the day, Jesus slept through the storm. Awakened by the frantic disciples, He rebuked the wind and the waves, calming the sea and the storm.

Soon afterward the evangelistic team arrived in Gadara, where a demon-possessed man immediately confronted Jesus. Jesus delivered the man and gave the demons permission to enter a herd of swine. The pigs were so intolerant of the devil that all of them committed suicide by drowning themselves in the sea!

It is here that we are introduced to a fully engaged dad. This man could have competed for the "father of the year" award. His name? Jairus. He was a ruler in the synagogue. Jairus made his way to Jesus because he had a daughter who was gravely ill. Having been chosen as a leader in his local synagogue, Jairus was obviously an upright man.

Listen to the desperation of this man: "He fell down at Jesus' feet and begged Him to come to his house, for he had an only daughter about twelve years of age, and she was dying" (Luke 8:41–42). Nothing is more frightening than having a child who is staring death in the whites of the eyes. In such a scenario a parent feels completely helpless. At a time like this the expectation of a parent is that everyone will do everything possible to save the life of that child. This is not an unrealistic expectation, for what could be more important? Yet in such times it often appears that not everything possible is being done to turn the situation around. Minutes feel like days, as everything seems to have gone into slow motion.

As Jesus began His walk to the humble house where Jairus's daughter lay at the point of death, a woman who had been sick as long as Jairus's daughter had been alive touched the hem of Jesus's garment and was instantly healed. Jesus engaged in a lengthy conversation with His disciples about who had touched Him. Jesus then turned His attention to the woman with the sickness—a problem that had caused her to hemorrhage for twelve years straight—and spoke to her about how her faith had made her whole.

As far as Jairus was concerned, critical time had slipped away. Can you imagine successfully getting in touch with the person who was the only hope for your daughter, only to see Him get interrupted with the needs of others? Jairus knew time was of the essence; in fact, his daughter died as a result of the delay caused when the woman with the issue of blood was healed! When one's child is lingering between life and death, time and resources are the quintessence of survival.

Those are the same emotions and concerns that faced the parents of Logan Knupp. Logan entered the world in March 1997 with a "sweet and easy-going" disposition, the second child to Alan and Lisa Knupp of Monroeville, Pennsylvania. Lisa, a kindergarten teacher at Cheswick Christian Academy, took time out of her career to enjoy being home with her two young sons. She knew that the greatest investment she could make in life was her children. Alan and Lisa understood that her being home with the children would necessitate some sacrifices, but they were willing to make the investment.

Eight months later Logan was the subject of great concern. Lisa noticed that her happy baby showed some odd behaviors. He had trouble sitting up; one of his eyes turned inward, toward the corner; he was becoming wobbly and had bouts of projectile vomiting.

Lisa took Logan to the family pediatrician, who found nothing wrong. Nonetheless he sent Logan on to a noted ophthalmologist to determine why his eye appeared to be turning inward. They were not expecting it to be anything serious.

The eye doctor told Lisa he didn't think there was anything to worry about, but when Lisa persisted, he scheduled Logan for an MRI at Children's Hospital of Pittsburgh. Instead of finding a weak eye muscle that would strengthen with time, the MRI showed a tumor the size of a Ping-Pong ball growing at the base of Logan's brain. The terror of that discovery cannot be described. Deep anguish washed over the young parents. The word *tumor* automatically struck fear; questions about Logan's future flooded their minds.

Alan and Lisa were in the MRI triage room with several family members when the doctor arrived with the test results. "Your son has a malignant brain tumor," he told them. "We recommend he stay here; we need to do surgery right away."

"The news shocked us," Alan says. As a parent, how do you prepare for such disastrous news? In the weight of the diagnosis, fear and sorrow so unbearable caused Alan to fall to the floor in complete shock.

Lisa began to call the family, making them aware of what they were facing and enlisting each of them to pray and to get others to pray. Alan and Lisa were absolutely convinced that prayer could change things. They believed the God they served could deliver a miracle to their young son.

The next day Lisa placed her tiny child into the hands of nurses who prepped Logan for emergency surgery. Gathered with Lisa's sister Lora, Alan's brother Paul, their pastors, and the doctor, Alan and Lisa asked God for a successful surgery. While the weight of the moment pressed in around them, they called on the One who could go where they could not go and do what they could not do; they believed God would guide the hands of the surgeon.

Then came the long wait. Minutes turned into hours as time seemed to stand still. Logan spent six long, agonizing hours in surgery as the medical team removed the tumor. Alan and Lisa passed the time praying and calling friends and family members with updates. It was the longest day of their lives.

GOOD NEWS AND BAD NEWS

In the operating room doctors found the tumor lying on the base of the brain and successfully removed 98 percent of it. Logan spent the night in the intensive care unit.

To make certain the surgery had found all the cancer, doctors ordered another MRI the following day. Alan and Lisa were waiting with Logan in the baby's hospital room when the entire neurology team came in to break the news: Logan's spinal cord was encased by a tumor that had wrapped itself around Logan's spine like an ivy vine. The prognosis was absolutely stunning and tragic: Logan had a one-in-ten chance to live to see his first birthday.

The news hit the young family like a ton of bricks. How could a thing like this happen? Surely this was a bad dream! They would wake up to find that none of this had really happened, wouldn't they? They prayed for this to be so, but despair settled over them.

"This was our low point," Alan says now. "We had been

encouraged with the results of the surgery; we had felt Logan would get a good report, but this news crushed us. We were both crying. The news of a tumor wrapped around his spine seemed to be the end."

The medical team revealed there was nothing they could do. The tumor on Logan's spine was inoperable. It appeared the only thing that could be done was for Alan and Lisa to make the most of whatever time Logan had left.

Alan and Lisa were told that with very aggressive chemotherapy Logan's life could possibly be prolonged. Because they wanted as much time with their son as possible, they agreed to extensive chemotherapy.

The neurology team sent the family home to rest before the chemo started. To their horror, they discovered that "Logan could not sleep because of the medications."

Alan remembers, "He was restless and clearly in pain. We laid him in the middle of the floor and had an Abraham moment; we lifted up our son in prayer to God."

Others were praying constantly too. Pastors came by to anoint the baby with oil and pray over him. Friends from church and work "stood guard" over the weary family, lifting them up in prayer and speaking encouraging words over them. Though doctors said Logan was beyond hope, an army of faith-filled believers held on to God, praying audaciously.

Though medical science is wonderful and has helped countless people, faith often goes beyond human experience to perform the impossible. This was the very thing family and friends of Alan and Lisa Knupp contended for in prayer! They believed God was going to raise up young Logan, and God alone would get the glory for the miracle.

Alan says his favorite passage of Scripture then was Psalm 91, and he latched on to its promises:

He who dwells in the secret place of the Most High shall abide under the shadow of the Almighty. I will say of the LORD, "He is my refuge and my fortress; my God, in Him I will trust." Surely He shall deliver you from the snare of the fowler and from the perilous pestilence. He shall cover you with His feathers, and under His wings you shall take refuge; His truth shall be your shield and buckler. You shall not be afraid of the terror by night, nor of the arrow that flies by day, nor of the pestilence that walks in darkness, nor of the destruction that lays waste at noonday. A thousand may fall at your side, and ten thousand at your right hand; but it shall not come near you. Only with your eyes shall you look, and see the reward of the wicked. Because you have made the LORD, who is my refuge, even the Most High, your dwelling place, no evil shall befall you, nor shall any plague come near your dwelling; for He shall give His angels charge over you, to keep you in all your ways. In their hands they shall bear you up, lest you dash your foot against a stone. You shall tread upon the lion and the cobra, the young lion and the serpent you shall trample underfoot. "Because he has set his love upon Me, therefore I will deliver him; I will set him on high, because he has known My name. He shall call upon Me, and I will answer him; I will be with him in trouble; I will deliver him and honor him. With long life I will satisfy him, and show him My salvation."

Fifteen times the word *shall* is used in this passage. The psalmist makes it very clear that God is on the case and working on our behalf. Alan and Lisa riveted their hope to this word and held on for dear life—the life of their young son Logan. They were not going to give up without a fight.

Despite their statement of unwavering faith, lab results were unable to determine the specific type of cancer affecting Logan; therefore doctors were not able to accurately determine what type of treatment to provide. His pathology reports were sent to several labs, but no one had a definitive diagnosis.

In what appeared to be a hopeless attempt to try everything possible for the youngster, the doctors said they would treat Logan for medulloblastoma, the most common form of cerebral tumors in children. Logan's treatment would consist of chemotherapy for the next three years, provided Logan survived that long. Radiation was ruled out because he was too young. In an attempt to prolong life as much as possible, the doctors pulled out the "big guns."

It was decided that chemotherapy would start on Sunday and go twenty-four hours a day for seven days. Logan would rest for a week, after which another round would begin. For a boy so young and for a family whose routines were turned upside down already, the schedule seemed impossible. It was immediately apparent that the treatment would be physically challenging for both Logan and his entire family.

Thankfully the Knupps had a marvelous church family and a network of friends. "They brought food, sent cards, and prayed all the time," Alan notes. "The elders of the church came by to anoint Logan with oil on numerous occasions. Others cleaned the house, bought groceries, and even repaired the furnace."

The following month a woman they knew as a "prayer warrior" came to see Logan's family. "Marty was the grandmother of one of Lisa's former students," Alan says. "She came to our home in Monroeville and told us she had a word from the Lord for Logan. Lisa knew in her spirit that the woman was for real, that her word was truly from God."

Marty told them God had shown her Logan's spine. "At the bottom of the spine was an ax, and the ax was lying down," she said. "The ax was a sign that God had cut away the tumor and had put down the ax to show His work was finished."

God had also revealed to her "two lighthouses shining their light over a large body of water." At the time the Knupps were not able to grasp all that the vision meant, "but we were believing God to bring it forth," Alan acknowledges.

It was a month after the initial diagnosis, during the second round of weeklong chemotherapy treatments, that the Knupps got some shocking news. After another MRI, the radiologist entered Logan's hospital room and told the family they could go home. Alan and Lisa were confused. They knew they had to stay the entire week for Logan's chemotherapy treatment.

"What about the tumor?" they asked. They questioned the radiologist, explaining about the tumor and the brain surgery, and saying they were certain they were to stay for more chemotherapy.

"What tumor?" asked the radiologist. "Your son is fine."

The Knupps were speechless. They didn't know what to say or ask.

Finally the radiologist asked permission from the parents to get the results from the previous scan in order to compare the two. Once the scans were placed side by side, the scans bore the proof. There was no tumor anywhere! The results revealed only a dark shadow at the bottom of the baby's spine. The Knupps believed this shadow was the "ax of God," laid down when Logan's healing was accomplished.

"OUR GOD CAN DO ALL THINGS"

The scan set off a stir. A team of doctors evaluated the results. No one could explain how a tumor that was supposed to claim Logan's life no longer existed. A doctor performed a spinal tap on Logan and reported "no sign of any tumor even at the cellular level." There was "*nothing*" on the baby's spine, he said. The tumor was completely gone! Logan was cancer free!

"Lisa's sister and brother-in-law were with us when we got the news," Alan says. "We were literally awed. No one knew what to say. Our God can do all things."

Logan continued to receive low-dose chemotherapy as part of a three-year protocol. Doctors advised it, and the Knupps agreed after prayer. "It was part of God's plan," Alan says.

Logan endured multiple blood and platelet transfusions, surgeries, flushes, fever watches, several eye surgeries, and a stem cell harvest. Lisa went with him on most trips to the hospital so Alan could keep working.

"Logan's a fighter," his dad says. "He responded well to it all. Of course, he lost his hair, and blood transfusions were common."

Seventeen months into the three-year protocol, Lisa received a word from the Lord that the chemotherapy must be stopped. The oncologist strongly recommended that an experimental plan of chemo treatments continue, but Lisa firmly said God was telling her to put it to an end.

The following day Logan was admitted to the hospital. Lisa was told by Logan's nurse that a new neuro-oncologist, one who shared her positive "faith," had joined the hospital staff.

After reviewing Logan's chart, the believing doctor said, "I don't see the need for more chemo." This was confirmation that God indeed wanted the chemo stopped. Logan was scheduled for a final MRI, which came back negative for any tumors.

"It was a long journey, and we were exhausted," Alan remembers. "Financially the Lord provided more than a million dollars for our medical bills. I remember paying only seventy dollars out of pocket."

Today Logan is fifteen years old and in the ninth grade. He enjoys playing hockey and basketball, playing Xbox 360, and going to youth group activities. He sings, loves to work at his part-time job, and has been described as "sensitive to others." His last MRI was in 2003. He has never had another tumor, and doctors say it is unlikely he ever will.

Alan and Lisa did not receive their miracle when they wanted it. They preferred to have it before the surgeons ever operated on Logan the first time. Our ways are not necessarily God's ways, and our timing is often not synchronized with God's time. But one thing is sure: if we can be patient, God will get to us in His time, and His timing is always perfect.

Jairus wanted Jesus to come and heal his daughter immediately, but Jesus squeezed another individual into His already hectic schedule as He made His way to where the dying daughter lay. I am sure Jairus was a bit on edge at the delay. Jairus knew how sick his daughter was; he knew that every second counted. Admittedly Jairus was probably not as interested in the miracle of the woman with the issue of blood as he was to move Jesus along so that his daughter could be healed.

Sure enough, Jairus was right; time slipped away for his daughter. Luke makes us aware that as Jesus was talking with the woman with the issue of blood, a messenger arrived with the tragic news that the young girl was dead. Jairus's heart must have collapsed within him and his knees become weak; his thoughts must have been racing.

"If this woman had not interrupted Jesus, my daughter would have been healed. Because of her miracle, I will have to plan a funeral," he may have thought.

The words of Jesus hit Jairus's thoughts like a shooting star through the night sky: "Do not be afraid; only believe, and she will be made well" (Luke 8:50).

Jesus must have read Jairus's thoughts. Because of the bad news, could he allow his hope to connect with the words of Jesus? Did he dare let his hopes be raised? The messenger said she was already

THE AUDACITY OF Prayer

dead. Could the healer stare down death and deliver a little girl out of its impious grasp?

Jairus decided to cast himself and the well-being of his family upon Jesus and believe death would lose its grip on his little girl. Alan and Lisa did the same thing. When they were told their son would never celebrate his first birthday, they decided to believe that God could rewrite the facts and cause their son to live a healthy and happy life.

Read the words of Jesus as He confronts the mourners who had already assembled at Jairus's home: "Do not weep; she is not dead, but sleeping" (Luke 8:52). The crowd took Jesus to task for His statement; He responded by asking them to leave the house. The only people remaining in the house with Him were Peter, James, John, Jairus, and his wife.

See how the miracle unfolded. "He... took her by the hand and called, saying, 'Little girl, arise.' Then her spirit returned, and she arose immediately. And He commanded that she be given something to eat. And her parents were astonished" (vv. 54–56).

The same God who healed Jairus's daughter healed Alan and Lisa Knupp's son Logan. The Scripture lets us know that God is "no respecter of persons" (Acts 10:34, KJV). What He has done for others, He will certainly do for us! If He was willing to heal the daughter of Jairus and Logan Knupp, He is willing to heal you!

Are you ready for your miracle? If so, will you pray the following prayer with me?

Dear Father, I place my difficulty [name your issue] before You. I have tried everything I know to fix this, and I cannot do it on my own. Others have done all they know to do, to no avail. I confess to You that the only way this is going to be resolved is for Your fingerprints to be on it. I give this over to You, believing a miracle is happening now. I curse the enemy and command him to flee the scene. You are a God of miracles, and I am a person of faith. Your Word says You will honor my faith, and I am confessing my miracle is happening now. I believe this to be Your will, and I am calling it done in Jesus's name. Amen.

Thirteen

CAN YOU HANDLE THIS?

ECOND TIMOTHY 1:11–12 says, "I was appointed a preacher, an apostle, and a teacher of the Gentiles. For this reason I also suffer these things; nevertheless I am not ashamed, for I know whom I have believed and am persuaded that He is able to keep what I have committed to Him until that Day."

The apostle Paul (then Saul) certainly had an interesting life. He began, by his own admission, as a religious bigot, living according to the demands of the Law, but persecuting the church. His religious training and personal piety could not allow for the truth of Christ as the Savior of the world. Because of this, he became the worst nightmare of the upstart Christians and this new message.

He made it his business to persecute both men and women, throw Christians in jail, and even see to the execution of many of them. He was a real-life tyrant who was wreaking havoc on the fledgling church headquartered in Jerusalem.

I am so glad God looks beyond who we are to see who we are capable of becoming. We all have some things in our past that we are not proud of and would like to place in the rearview mirror of life. Saul was certainly a person who needed a lot of forgiveness before he could go forward with God. The good news is that God offers as much forgiveness as necessary.

Saul was on his way to Damascus with arrest warrants to seize a new wave of Christians and throw them in jail when he met someone more powerful than he. Prior to his visit, he had sent word that he intended to do much harm to those who professed to be followers of Christ. Christians were terrified of him, and though they were not ashamed to share their faith, they were filled with great trepidation when this man's name came up in a conversation.

Before Saul's arrival in Damascus, God intervened for the church and in the life of this very wicked and hateful man. One of the greatest transformations ever to happen to a human being happened just outside Damascus. God struck Saul from his transportation with a blinding light and an audible word from heaven. Right then and there Saul recognized what was transpiring and turned to God, disposed of his arrest warrants, and followed Jesus. He became known as the apostle Paul, and his letters make up much of the New Testament.

Because of his conversion Paul spent the great balance of his life moving from jail cell to jail cell and being under suspicion by the church. Yet from that day on the road to Damascus until the time of his death, he never wavered from the message of Christ.

The persecution Paul experienced was almost unbearable. He wrote in his letter to the church at Corinth:

> I have worked harder and have been put in jail more times. I have been beaten with whips more and have been in danger of death more often. Five times the Jews gave me thirty-nine lashes with a whip. Three times the Romans beat me with a big stick, and once my enemies stoned me. I have been shipwrecked three times, and I even had to spend a night and a day in the sea. During my many travels, I have been in danger from rivers, robbers, my own people, and foreigners. My life has been in danger in cities, in deserts, at sea, and with people who only pretended to be the Lord's followers. I have worked and struggled and spent many sleepless nights.

I have gone hungry and thirsty and often had nothing to eat. I have been cold from not having enough clothes to keep me warm. Besides everything else, each day I am burdened down, worrying about all the churches.

—2 Corinthians 11:23–28, cev

Though Paul suffered many things at the hands of many people, he never allowed his faith to waver. He stood his ground, preached the Word, and maintained the integrity of his testimony despite all that the enemy threw at him. The same is true of Gail Benedickson (formerly Manning), whose son Paul was born on July 14, 1969, at Baldwin Hills Hospital in Baldwin Hills, California.

"From the very first time the nurses brought him to me for his regular feedings, I sensed something was wrong," Gail remembers.

The baby's breathing appeared very labored, especially when his mother attempted to feed him. His coloring was not normal, either. Little Paul's complexion was very olive, and he was blue or purple around his mouth, hands, and feet. Besides his labored breathing, he choked while trying to nurse his bottle. This ordeal was extremely frightening for a young mom who loved her child with all her heart.

Gail said, "I tried to share my concerns with the nurses at the hospital, but I was assured that all was well." Even though Gail and her husband recognized something was terribly wrong, the medical staff did not seem to be overly concerned. In fact, they were quite dismissive.

Three days after giving birth, Gail was discharged to go home. On that particular morning the family physician who delivered Paul came to talk to Gail and her husband. Gail remembers, "He told us that he, along with other doctors and nurses on staff, were concerned about Paul's condition. It seemed that after I had voiced my concerns, they had been observing little Paul more closely and now felt he needed to be moved to Children's Hospital in Los Angeles—and the move needed to take place immediately."

The doctor was not able to tell the Mannings what was wrong with Paul but said he felt it might be life-threatening, possibly something as serious as spinal meningitis. He wanted Paul admitted to a hospital that was better equipped to deal with his medical condition, where more extensive testing could properly identify the problem.

WEIGHING THE RISKS

Paul's parents were in agreement, so the child was moved to the ICU pediatrics ward on the sixth floor of Children's Hospital in Los Angeles that very morning. Once there he was placed in an oxygenated isolate with more electro probes connected to his little body than he had skin to handle.

Gail said, "We were not allowed to touch or handle him at all. His isolate was equipped with large rubber gloves that we put on from the outside, which allowed us to touch him through the gloves. No skin-to-skin touching was allowed."

Paul's breathing was very erratic; his little chest would ripple like the waves of the ocean. There were many moments when the young parents watched their son with great fear, thinking he might stop breathing altogether. The seconds between breaths seemed far too long, and his every breath was extremely labored.

Paul was probed and pricked many times during his stay at the Los Angeles hospital. It seemed that every day Paul's parents were told something different based on the most recent tests. At first the medical team thought Paul might have a blood disorder stemming from genetics, so for days they tested Gail to see if there was any underlying blood disorder that was affecting the baby. He was subjected to a series of X-rays and EKGs, multiple CBC and urine tests, a PKU test, and a bacteriological test. The CBC is a complete blood count test that checked the hemoglobin, hematocrit, and red blood cell counts in Paul's blood. The PKU test is the standard phenylketonuria test performed routinely today on newborns. It is used to determine if a baby has the enzyme needed for normal growth and development. The absence of the enzyme can cause phenylalanine in the baby's blood to rise, which can cause brain damage and seizures. The bacteriological test was used to determine the levels of particular bacteria in his little body.

Nothing alarming was found in these blood tests, which left the medical team confused. The probing continued.

On Friday, after a week in the Los Angeles hospital, Paul's parents were told definitively that their baby had a hole in his heart and needed a heart catheterization. Gail remembers, "At that point we had never heard of such a thing, and the news was devastating!"

The head cardiologist explained that the hole compromised little Paul's circulatory system. As his small heart pumped, his blood flow on one side of his body was restricted and backing up, causing him to suffocate, while on the other side he was drowning in his own blood. The opening caused Paul's heart to work strenuously in an effort to compensate.

The only remedy, the cardiologist said, was the catheterization, which was an invasive surgery to close the hole. He explained the procedure to Gail and her husband, along with the life-threatening risks involved. The doctor was brutally honest, saying, "For a baby so young, so tiny, any slip or deviation might result in his death." There were no guarantees with the surgery, but it was almost certain that Paul would not survive without it.

"At that time my husband and I were active members of Faith Center in Glendale where Ray Schock was senior pastor," Gail said. "Pastor Schock's was a ministry that prayed for and believed God to do the miraculous." The church had a Christian radio and TV broadcasting network that beamed across southern California.

Through the radio and television ministry, prayer went up literally 24/7 for God to intervene and heal Paul.

The cardiac surgeon was scheduled to perform the heart catheterization on Paul the following Monday and explained again the high risk involved due to Paul's tiny size. "Remember, the baby's heart was the size of a walnut," Gail says. "Slipping a wire through a tiny blood vessel and into his heart was virtually impossible back then. The doctor said Paul was as fragile as a wet paper bag. One slip of the hand and our son would be dead."

After much prayer and weighing the risks involved, the Mannings elected to trust God rather than having the surgery. They realized the risks and decided to take their chances on God rather than the doctor, who seemed so unsure about such a risky surgical procedure. That very same day there seemed to be some improvements. Paul's breathing seemed more relaxed; his coloring improved a bit.

"Doctors and nurses were in constant communication with us over the weekend. Paul began to take a turn for the better, they said. His coloring was improving. Our hopes and faith were energized, and we shared our praise report with family and church friends.

"On Saturday and Sunday the hospital staff said that if Paul continued to improve, we would get a call by seven Monday morning, and we could pick up our son. We received no further calls overnight, so early Monday morning, I sent my husband off to work, believing I would hear a good report from the doctor at any moment. No call came. At ten o'clock I phoned my husband at work to see if he had heard anything. Unknown to me, he had.

"He told me that on the Friday night before we had left the hospital for home, our doctors had convinced him to sign an authorization form for surgery—just in case Paul took a nosedive. In fact, Paul had taken a turn for the worse at ten o'clock Sunday evening.

We had not been contacted at that point; otherwise, we would have hurried to the hospital!

"But my husband had heard from the hospital that morning. Unknown to me, he had received two calls, both describing Paul's fight for breath and insisting on surgery. A nurse let him know the doctor was preparing to take Paul into the operating room for the catheterization."

Gail says, "I flipped my cork over this! I reminded my husband of all the prayers that had gone up for Paul and how we had agreed to trust God—and how in the world could he have done this thing behind my back and not tell me! I demanded he get the doctor on the phone *right then* and tell him *not* to do surgery on my baby!"

My husband said, "Look, Gail, Paul was scheduled for seven, and it's now almost ten. No one is going to answer that call." Gail says, "I didn't care; he needed to call the doctor *now!*"

He consented and called the hospital. At the time of his call, the doctor was scrubbing for our Paul's surgery when he was called to the phone in the operating room. As God would have it, Gail recalls, "We learned that Paul's surgery had been postponed due to another emergency. My husband told the doctor we did not want them doing surgery on Paul. There were to be no procedures, no nothing."

Frustrated, the doctor asked, "Well, if you are not going to let us do what we know to be right for your son, what do you want us to do?"

Not knowing what to say, Mr. Manning said, "I don't know. I guess just watch him and do what you can short of a surgical procedure."

"Then come to get your son!" the doctor said angrily.

When the Mannings arrived at the hospital, they were ushered into a conference room filled with pediatric doctors, surgeons, and heart specialists. Chaplains from every religion available were present, voicing opinions about how remiss and reckless it would be to refuse surgery and remove Paul from the hospital. The doctors and the hospital staff had taken the posture that the parents had to either consent to surgery or take the child out of their care and facility. The Mannings understood the liability of the doctor and hospital but felt surgery was not right for their son and were willing to take a leap of faith to prove it.

At one point during the confrontation, the head of pediatrics began explaining the ramifications of removing Paul out of ICU and taking him off of his oxygen. He described the different stages of "turning blue then purple then black" and how Paul would start gasping for air and eventually suffocate. His question to Gail shot through the room like a high-voltage electrical charge, "When all of this begins to happen—*and it will*—what are you going to do then, Mrs. Manning? Pray some more?"

Gail says, "Needless to say, his question triggered my righteous indignation. I told the doctor that I totally respected his medical expertise and was thankful that God had gifted him so with his divine brilliance. However, I said, you have told me you cannot guarantee the life of my son if we allow you to do this procedure. You have told me how very risky and complicated it is; therefore, I choose to place my baby in the hands of the Creator who gave him life, and whether God chooses to heal my son or take him to heaven does not negate God's power to heal, deliver, and set free!"

TAKING AUTHORITY

At that juncture the Mannings were asked to sign a release stating that they were taking their son from the hospital against the medical advice of the doctors and hospital staff. They were required to sign paperwork releasing the hospital from responsibility given their decision to take Paul home. They signed the form and prepared to be discharged from the hospital.

A member of the hospital staff accompanied Paul and his parents as they were leaving the hospital. Gail remembers, "While we were in the elevator going down from the sixth floor to the lobby, Paul began to do just as the doctors had said he would do. His little chest began to quiver at every breath he attempted to take. It was like that ocean roaring again. His color turned blue then purple. I looked at my husband, and he looked at me. Then he reached into the bassinet and placed his hand on Paul's little chest. As he did, Paul's tiny right hand reached up and grasped his daddy's hand while my husband prayed. 'Devil, you are a liar! I bind you in the name of Jesus. We are taking this baby out of here, dead or alive!' he prayed aloud."

The car was waiting at the curb; Mr. Manning opened the passenger-side door for Paul and his mom. The orderly placed Paul, bundled tightly, into the arms of his mother.

Gail said, "The instant the orderly took his hands off Paul, I witnessed God's life-giving source flow into my son! His skin pigmentation went from black and blue to the most beautiful white, rosy-colored flesh I had ever seen. His breathing immediately became normal! The ocean waves had been rebuked!"

Prior to being discharged from the hospital, Paul was scheduled for a follow-up appointment to have a chest X-ray. Gail felt a definite check in her spirit not to take Paul back to the hospital. She canceled the appointment. "They wanted him for experimental research," she said. "I was not going back."

Once home Paul was placed in his crib for the very first time. Gail recalls, "He peered up at us and smiled. Tears of joy and gratitude streamed down my face.

"Bringing our son home from the hospital was a huge relief," Gail said. "Being able to hold my son and care for him and his needs was gratifying. From his first night home I never once experienced any doubt or fear. God gave me perfect peace over him. He slept through the night and had a healthy appetite."

Several weeks later the Mannings received an unexpected visit from someone they believed to be from the hospital, checking up on Paul's needs. Gail said, "In actuality my visitor was from the Los Angeles County Welfare Department, Division of Children's Health and Welfare. We were being investigated!"

She said, "I answered every question. I showed my guest our wonderful, healthy son and let him bounce around on my knee. I told the woman what I was feeding him, how he was gaining weight, and how delighted we were to have him home at last."

In the report of that visit, the caseworker noted in writing that, "Paul appeared to be doing well. Mrs. Manning states that the baby has been touched by God." Case closed!

Paul had his first pediatrics checkup at about eight months old with a doctor who knew nothing of his history. "The doctor's first comment to me was, 'My, what a strong heart he has!'"

It was a comment Gail heard many times through Paul's childhood years. Paul grew normally. He was all boy. He loved sports and played hard. Today he is a living, breathing witness that God can close the hole in a heart in an instant of time without a surgical scar.

Paul is now forty-three. For the past sixteen years he has been employed with the federal government and is required to have a complete physical annually. He has never been told anything other than that he has a very strong heart!

On his birthday every year Gail shares the story of Paul's amazing healing. It may be in a church service or over a cup of coffee with a friend. She said, "Every birthday has been a celebration of what our powerful God can do for anyone who will ask and can believe Him. Praise the Lord for His mighty handiwork!"

The Mannings faced down the monster of death in their son's

life. Some would say that what they did was high risk and maybe a little unwise, but they decided that if they were going to take the risk of putting their son's life into someone's hands, it would be into hands scarred by nails.

Empowered by the Holy Spirit and his steadfast determination to do more good for the kingdom of God than he had perpetuated damage upon it, the apostle Paul stared down many enemies:

- He was in jail many times.

- He received 195 stripes with a whip.

- Three times the Romans beat him with a stick.

- Once he was stoned by those who hated him because of the gospel.

- He spent a night and a day in the wide-open sea.

- He suffered through three separate shipwrecks.

- He faced down many other crisis situations.

Yet, listen to these words, "None of these things move me; nor do I count my life dear to myself, so that I may finish my race with joy, and the ministry which I received from the Lord Jesus, to testify to the gospel of the grace of God" (Acts 20:24).

What are you struggling with? Can you say with the Manning family and the apostle Paul that you are going to put your trust in God and believe Him to deliver on His promises?

After enumerating the difficulties one might encounter in our journey from the nursery to the grave, the apostle appears to mock his problems and tormentors when he says, "For our light affliction, which is but for a moment, worketh for us a far more exceeding and eternal weight of glory; while we look not at the things which are seen, but at the things which are not seen: for the things which are seen are temporal; but the things which are not seen are eternal" (2 Cor. 4:17–18, KJV).

Think about this: after all Paul had gone through, he calls his difficulties "light affliction." How could this be? He was able to make this statement of unwavering faith because he was personally acquainted with the God who was dedicated to bringing him through his most difficult trial. He was also viewing his problems in light of eternity.

When facing death with their son, the Mannings discovered what the apostle Paul knew: there is no power greater than God's power! They decided to take the hand of God and the hand of their son and charge bravely into the future. God did not let them down, and He will not let you down.

Would you take God by the hand today and believe Him for your greatest need? He stands ready to make your future possible. Pray this prayer with me:

> *Dear Lord, please help my unbelief. The trials of life have just about destroyed my faith in You, but today I am coming back. I am going to get up from this mat of despair and charge boldly into the future You have for me. You are greater than the trial I face, and I give my situation to You, believing that You are going to work it out. I commit to leave this in Your hands and never to take it into my hands again. I will expectantly await the resolution of this matter and give You the glory for the good result I know is about to transpire. You are greater than all that has befallen me, and I give You praise, in Jesus's name. Amen.*

Fourteen

CAN GOD BIRTH FAITH AND JOY?

ONE OF THE best-known passages in the Bible is Psalm 23. This passage is recognizable to almost every person on the planet who claims to be a Christian. Though frequently quoted and recited, the contents of the chapter are often missed almost entirely.

The reference point of this chapter is that God is depicted as the Good Shepherd, and we are in the role of the sheep. The psalmist declares God to be the provider who is constantly looking for the best pastures for the sheep to graze in. Notice that the sheep do not decide where they are going to forage; the shepherd makes that decision.

The sheep left to themselves would nibble the grass down to the point that the ground would become sterile and nonproductive. But the eye of the shepherd is constantly searching the countryside for a field of green grass that has a year-round brook where the sheep can eat and drink their fill.

The field of choice for the shepherd must also be situated perfectly where the least risk is posed to the well-being of the sheep. True shepherds place their personal and professional well-being on the back burner in preference to the sheep. Conversely, hirelings fleece the sheep and flee at the first sign of danger, leaving the flock in peril of their very lives.

All of us are called to be a shepherd of some kind. Political leaders shepherd nations and municipalities; proprietors shepherd workforces; pastors shepherd church folks; and parents shepherd their families. Both Ezekiel and Jeremiah prophesied, "Woe to the shepherds" who misuse and abuse the flock they are responsible for leading (Ezek. 34:2; Jer. 23:1). God takes a very dim view of those who use leadership to their own advantage and the hurt of everyone else.

One thing everyone in the shepherding business has in common is the encountering of danger. At one time or another every leader must face down danger and remain brave and decisive despite the overwhelming emotion to flee the scene. The psalmist David faced repeated moments of fright and the desire to take flight during his storied career as a shepherd and king. Listen to his words here in Psalm 23:4: "Yea, though I walk through the valley of the shadow of death, I will fear no evil; for You are with me."

David was no stranger to danger. With his bare hands he killed a lion and bear while protecting his flock. During his forty-year reign as king he dismantled the forces of other nations who attacked Israel. He outlasted the efforts of his own son who created a mutiny and attempted a hostile takeover.

Danger? Yes, David was well acquainted with danger. Listen how he relates to the dangerous circumstances of life: "I walk through the valley of the shadow of death" (v. 4). Think of this: when danger exists, it is much easier to run than walk. We want to get through danger as quickly as possible, so our pace in dangerous times is more often hurried. Yet because we run rather than walk, we miss some of what God has for us to learn in the "valley of the shadow of death."

We must always remember that when we are called upon to go through a thing, there is something for us to learn. There is a purpose much higher than we are capable of knowing. Such was the case for Tim and Angie Todd.

Tim Todd gets around. For more than twenty-five years he and his wife, Angie, have traveled the planet as evangelists, telling audiences about the goodness of God and watching God's miraculous power of salvation and restoration touch thousands of lives. And since 1996 they have shared the most amazing story of God's supernatural touch on their own family.

Their remarkable story began during a revival Tim and Angie were conducting in Kailua, Hawaii. One night Angie woke from a troubled sleep. She'd had a dream about the baby. In Angie's dream James Dobson was on the radio when Angie gave birth to a stillborn baby, and he said, "There is someone listening who needs a miracle for their baby." As soon as Angie heard those words, she lifted her baby into the air and cried out to God. The Lord responded by raising her baby from the dead, and Angie named the child Miracle Joy. Tim remembers, "Angie awakened me and with a trembling voice told me the details of her dream."

Tim and Angie were walking in the center of God's will. Tim had followed his father, Cecil Todd, into the ministry, and he and his wife had dedicated themselves to service. In October 1994 Angie had given birth to Timothy "Luke" Todd with no complications. In fact, Tim remembers, "We arrived at the hospital at 7:52 in the morning, and Luke was born at 7:59; every mother's dream!"

Even so, with Luke's recent birth fresh in their memories, the couple took note of Angie's dream. They had no way of knowing what the dream was about, but they were confident the Lord would reveal the meaning in His time.

"Six months later we learned we were expecting again," Tim recalls. "We were elated." Dutifully Angie reported in for her initial doctor's visit. After a routine ultrasound a nurse asked, "How do you feel about having two?"

"Well," Angie answered, "Luke is a good baby, and Tim and I are ready for a second child."

The nurse looked up. "No," she said. "You are pregnant with two *now*."

The family obstetrician finished his examination and calculated the delivery date. Though Angie was still early in the "timeline," the doctor recognized that the two babies were very small. He wrote her a referral for her to visit a perinatologist to see why the babies were so tiny.

Tim and Angie were soon meeting Dr. Edward Neuman, who practiced in their hometown of Baton Rouge, Louisiana. Dr. Neuman took Angie in for extensive ultrasounds and confirmed that the babies were, indeed, too small for their age.

The doctor writes, "After I saw Angela and performed ultrasounds on the fetuses, we found that they were severely discordant. Mariah Faith was roughly twice the size of the smaller fetus, Miracle Joy. When you have severely discordant fetuses like this, and especially when the smallest twin has no amniotic fluid around it, which was the case for Miracle Joy, then a condition called twin-to-twin transfusion syndrome is diagnosed. When the condition is diagnosed as early as it was in Angela (at twenty-two weeks gestational age), the prognosis is inevitably poor for both children."

Dr. Neuman said he was alarmed because of Angie's dangerous symptoms. "We were told that one of the twins was at least twice the size of the other, and both were far too small for their gestational age," Tim says. To make matters worse, the smallest baby was stuck against the wall of Angie's womb.

Dr. Neuman, who was not a believer, shook his head. "There is a 95 to 100 percent chance of these fetuses dying in the womb by the twenty-eighth week or earlier," he said. He recommended that Angie terminate the pregnancy. This was the beginning of a walk through the valley of the shadow of death for this young couple.

Could they walk through this valley, or would they take flight and run for their lives? Though they experienced all the emotions every other parent in this situation would face, they believed God would lead them along the path to birth Faith and Joy!

This believing couple remembered the dream that had startled Angie months earlier in Hawaii and recognized it as a word from God. They believed Angie's dream of giving birth to a stillborn baby and the child being raised from the dead was a signal from God that though the report was bleak, God would give life to what the doctors thought was certain death.

"Because of that dream the previous October, we knew God was going to spare the life of our twins," Tim says.

So when Dr. Neuman gave them the bad news and recommended aborting the babies, Angie looked at him and said, "With all due respect, what you have just said went in one ear and out the other. We will walk out of the hospital with both of our twins alive."

BELIEVING FOR A MIRACLE

At home they got on the phone to parents on both sides of the family, their pastor, and some close friends, requesting prayer for the miracle they knew God was intending to give them. They never allowed doubt to push out faith; they were going to take a stroll through the valley of the shadow of death and emerge with Faith and Joy!

With each subsequent visit they found the discordance progressively worsening. The smaller twin, Miracle Joy, continued to have no amniotic fluid around her body. There was little chance either fetus would survive. The babies were rejecting nutrition in the womb.

"God had given us the faith to believe," Tim states. "Our faith was strong for a miracle. I would pray with Angie and for the twins. I constantly held her close and spoke the Word of God over her and to her womb."

Tim and Angie held on to the promise written in 1 Peter 2:24: "By [His] stripes you were healed." Tim and Angie understood exactly what the apostle Peter was saying; the healing is past tense because it had already been done. If the healing had already been done, all they had to do was stroll through the valley of the shadow of death and emerge with Faith and Joy!

The couple also drew comfort by quoting Nehemiah 8:10: "The joy of the LORD is your strength." They decided the enemy was not going to steal the zest from their journey, and they would literally give birth to Faith and Joy!

Tim says, "Throughout this pregnancy, even in the midst of getting bad reports from the doctor, we had an overwhelming joy that only God can give."

Together they found the certainty of Romans 8:28 a rock for their faith: "And we know that all things work together for good to those who love God, to those who are the called according to His purpose."

"After one of the many doctor visits where we were given another death sentence, I went to my vehicle wondering why God had not already given us a miracle of growth for the twins in the womb," Tim says. "I knew God was going to come through, but I had in mind that the twins were going to grow supernaturally while they were still in the womb. After all, we had strong faith, and knowing that godly people full of faith all over the world were praying for these twins, there appeared to be no reason for the unborn girls not to be healed before birth.

"Sitting in the car, I prayed, 'God, you are a *now* God, and I claim healing for our twins *now*, in Jesus's name.' When I finished praying, God spoke to my heart and said, 'Tim, are you through?'

"Yes, Lord."

"He said, 'Now do you want to do this, or do you want Me to do this?'"

"I said, 'Lord, I want You to do this.'"

"'Tim,' He answered, 'I am accomplishing something bigger than what you can see.'"

Tim and Angie stood on the solid ground of that word from the Lord for the rest of the pregnancy. As they walked though their personal valley of the shadow of death, they were not going to allow the enemy to strike fear in their hearts and start a stampede. They would calmly walk the path they had been called upon to travel. Walking rather than running through our difficulty signals faith rather than fear, and God responds to faith in a very positive manner.

They did not terminate the pregnancy. They believed in the sanctity of life. Besides, God had confirmed to them through a dream that the prediction of death would come, but a birth would occur. They went forward, trusting God to bring reality to the hope He had deposited in their hearts.

On August 31, 1996, Angela underwent a primary Cesarean section. Miracle Joy was born first, weighing in at one pound. "She was vigorous," her dad remembers. "She had an excellent cry, good active motion, and a normal heart rate."

Then came Mariah Faith, born two minutes later, weighing two pounds, fourteen ounces, also in excellent health. Tim and Angie were overwhelmed with joy. God had answered their prayers, though dark hours still lay ahead.

The most difficult time came three weeks later. Miracle Joy had dropped from her birth weight of a mere one pound to twelve ounces. Doctors had run out of veins for IVs. Dr. Neuman informed them that they were going to have to perform a central line placement, an invasive surgery to place a small tube in Miracle Joy's chest so she could receive transfusions and nutrition.

Miracle Joy came through the surgery, but at three in the morning Tim and Angie got an alarming phone call from the hospital. The messenger said they had "completely lost Miracle Joy's heart rate and blood pressure," Tim remembers. "They had given her a shot to stimulate her body, and it didn't work. They had performed chest compressions with their thumbs and were able to revive her, but said she might not make it through the night. We were told we needed to get to the hospital immediately if we wanted to see her."

Rushing in minutes later, Tim and Angie saw their daughter's ashen body. "I reached in to touch her. The doctor caught my wrist and stopped me because the least bit of stimulation could cause her to have cardiac arrest.

"My heart broke for her," Tim continues. "As I looked at her with needles and tubes in her head, arms, legs, belly, and other places, the Lord spoke to my heart. 'Tim, you are experiencing in a very small way what I went through when I had to leave My beloved Son hanging on a cross. I did not hold Him when He needed Me most. I left Him there to save you.'"

Only because of the hand of God holding her did Miracle Joy make it through those long hours. The next day passed; a week flew by. She continued to struggle. She could eat only with a feeding tube; she continued to require oxygen for breath. She endured six major operations and ten blood transfusions. But she didn't succumb; she fought for dear life.

Mariah Faith's story was different. After a week in the neonatal intensive care unit, she went home with no difficulties. Miracle Joy continued her hour-by-hour, day-by-day battle for life for five long months.

"There was never a 'turning point,'" Tim says, "only a gradual progression. Miracle Joy made slow, gradual progress. She kept us believing, trusting, holding on to our promises."

Three weeks after birth the doctor agreed that both twins were going to survive. The news of the hospital finally matched the promise of the Great Physician. The walk through the valley of the shadow of death was almost complete for the Todd family.

"We received a call from Dr. Neuman's secretary," Tim recalls. The doctor had written a letter stating, "I must admit I was rather hesitant to mix the field of medicine with religion. However, after monitoring this pregnancy for roughly ten weeks and seeing the outcome, I felt this does warrant consideration as the most outstanding medical miracle I have seen since I have been in practice."

Tim remembers, "When I went to pick up the letter, his secretary told me something I'll never forget. She said, 'Brother Todd, I've worked for Dr. Neuman for more than twenty years, and he has never allowed us to talk about God in the office. However, since your twins were born, all he talks about is the miracle God performed in your girls. Dr. Neuman told me to tell you that if you read this letter in your home church, he will come to the service to listen to you read it. That's another miracle,' she said. 'Dr. Neuman doesn't serve God and doesn't attend church.'"

Of course Tim made all the necessary arrangements, and one Sunday morning soon after, Dr. Neuman, his wife, and their four young children appeared in the congregation of the Todds' home church. Tim read the letter and then took a seat beside Dr. Neuman as the pastor ministered.

At home following the service, the phone rang in the Todd household. When Angie answered, to her surprise Dr. Neuman was on the line. He expressed to Angie that he had been raised in church as a little boy. When he began medical school, he got as far away from God as a person could get. He hadn't served God for more than twenty-eight years, but said, "Your twin girls have had such an impact on my life that on the way home from church, my wife and I made a decision to get our priorities straight with the Lord and serve Him."

Only then was it apparent why they had been called upon to walk not run through the valley of the shadow of death with their precious daughters. We must remember that God is more concerned with the outcome than He is with our personal, temporary comfort.

When Angie was talking to Dr. Neuman on the phone, the Todds remembered what the Lord had said to Tim months earlier: *"I am doing something bigger than what you can see."* God had used their walk through the valley of the shadow of death not only to heal the twins but also to bring the doctor and his family to faith in Christ.

A STEP OF FAITH

At the five-month mark Dr. Neuman told Tim and Angie they could take their daughter home. He said, "Miracle Joy is growing very slowly, but we have done all we can do for her at the hospital. It is time for you to take her home."

Finally the family was united. No more long hours apart with one or both parents at the hospital. But God had even more grace to bestow.

The Todd family's medical bills had piled up in excess of half a million dollars. The $65,000 insurance policy they had was depleted within the first two days. This financial responsibility on a traveling evangelist's salary was a heavy burden to bear.

Tim remembers, "On October 11 I was praying specifically about these enormous bills when God spoke to my heart again, very plainly, and instructed me to step out in faith and plant a seed of one thousand dollars in a mission project."

"I said, 'Lord, with all these medical bills, there's no way I can afford to give a thousand dollars to missions right now.' But God had a comeback. He said, 'Tim, with all these medical bills, there is no way you can afford not to give one thousand dollars to missions right now.'"

So, while trusting God for his own needs, Tim dropped a check in the mail that morning for the missions project. The very same day the mail brought another stack of medical bills to add to the pile already on his desk. There, in the middle of the stack, he found a letter from the director of the hospital's business office.

Tim tells the story: "She had taken it upon herself to contact all our medical carriers: the heart doctor, the lung doctor, the brain doctor, the pathologists, the hospital—everybody. All had agreed to write off the entire bill! She wrote, 'The Miracle Todd Twins have been the talk of the hospital!'"

Two precious, healthy babies, surrounded at home by a loving family and a miraculous deliverance from medical debt—could God add even more wonders to this awesome story? He did when he added another child, Mikalen Hope, born healthy and whole just three days before the twins turned one year old.

Today the Todd twins are seventeen years old. They love God. They sing and play the piano and perform in dramas at their home church in West Monroe, Louisiana. Tim and Angie watch in amazement as their twins participate in ball games at their Christian school. The family travels together to services during the summer. Miracle Joy and Mariah Faith are making good grades in high school.

The Todds have remained in contact with Dr. Neuman, even having dinner together occasionally. Today he and his wife and their four grown children are serving God because someone walked rather than ran through the valley of the shadow of death. God used the difficult birth of the twins to do *"something bigger than you can see."*

Tim says, "I share our story everywhere I go, and God uses it to build the faith of individuals who need miracles in their own lives. I remind them that in one experience, God provided a miracle of healing, finances, and salvation."

He continues, "Sometimes God allows us to go through trials to accomplish the things He desires." One thing is for sure, the Todd family believes, "God answers the fervent prayer of the righteous."

The psalmist David declared what the Todds had to live: "I will fear no evil; for You are with me" (Ps. 23:4). Fear is a difficult emotion to overcome when the pressure is on and the devil is screaming insults into our ears. But we must remember, fear is the enemy of faith, and if we are going to emerge victorious, faith must rule the day!

How could David be so confident about his stroll through the valley of the shadow of death? I believe the answer lies in David's shepherding experience. He knew a good shepherd never leaves the sheep, no matter what! He says as much in verse 4 of Psalm 23: "You are with me." David knew God was not going to leave his side, and the Todd family found that to be true as well. If the Lord remained with the psalmist and with the Todd family through their greatest battles of life, He will remain with you through your present circumstance.

Notice the words of David at the end of verse 4: "Your rod and Your staff, they comfort me." These words were not lost on David's audience. They knew well what the standard operating equipment of a shepherd looked like. The rod was a crude club, intended for anything or anyone who dared to attack the flock. The staff was a very long pole used for corralling and directing the sheep.

He makes this statement: "They comfort me." Who are they? They are the club and the long pole! When we encounter the most serious crisis of our lives and we feel completely alone, we must remember we are never alone! The Good Shepherd will never leave us alone. Not only will He be with us, but He also carries two big sticks and is ready to use one of them on our enemies and the other to direct our steps so we will arrive safely at the place of our miracle.

The Todd family had the audacity to pray and believe God for a miracle, and the psalmist David did the same on numerous occasions. The common denominator is that God showed up in a big way for them both, and He will do the same for you.

Can you give birth to faith and joy? The answer is a resounding *yes*!

If you are walking through your own personal valley of the shadow of death, please pray this prayer with me:

Dear Lord Jesus, I am traveling a lonely road in this season of my life. Everywhere I look there is death and destruction. Fear threatens to overtake me, but I choose to place my trust in You. I believe You are in this valley with me, and because of that, I will fear no evil. I know You will fight for me, even when I feel completely defenseless. I believe Your rod and staff are being used to my benefit even as I pray this prayer. Use Your rod on my enemy, and direct my every step with Your staff. By faith I speak my miracle into existence! With my eyes of faith I see it coming to pass! It will happen! You will bruise Satan under my feet momentarily! I give you praise for my miracle, in Jesus's name. Amen.

Fifteen

CAN GOD STRAIGHTEN ME UP?

*I*N LUKE 13 Jesus and His disciples attend the synagogue on the Sabbath. Nothing seemed out of the ordinary, as Jesus was accustomed to faithful church attendance and keeping the Sabbath Day holy. We know this based on Luke 4:16: "Jesus went back to Nazareth, where he had been brought up, and as usual he went to the meeting place on the Sabbath" (CEV).

I am not sure how many times Jesus had been to this very synagogue, but because He had been raised in Nazareth, probably too many times to count. Even so this Sabbath would turn out very differently from others because a woman was going to have her life changed that day.

During the course of the normal religious activities, Jesus had an opportunity to teach. With all attention focused on Him, He did something that upset the ruler of the synagogue. During His teaching Jesus noticed a woman who was stooped over. Her condition was so noticeable that Scripture states that she could not straighten herself up (Luke 13:11).

The passage does not say the woman was demon-possessed, only that a spirit of infirmity had afflicted her for the previous eighteen years. Think of this: for eighteen years this woman had been afflicted with spinal problems. Her condition had grown so grave she could not even stand upright, not even for a second or two.

I am sure this lady had consulted everyone she knew in an attempt to ascertain what was going on with her. In the beginning she probably thought the condition would quickly pass. Perhaps she got up each morning assuming her condition would disappear as mysteriously as it had appeared. But day after day she was disappointed to discover she was worse rather than better.

For eighteen long years this had been her ordeal. Eighteen years is a long time to deal with any condition, but to deal with back and spinal problems for such a long stretch of time is almost unbearable. At some point I am sure she came to believe this was to be her plight in life. Once she lost hope of a cure, she likely decided to make the best of her bad situation and do what she could to lead as normal a life as possible.

It is interesting to me that this story occurred in Nazareth, Jesus's hometown. This woman had heard about the miracles of Jesus, had she not? Why had she not come forward sooner and asked Jesus to heal her? The answer can probably be found in what the Scriptures say about the attitudes that prevailed in Nazareth about the miracle-working power of Jesus:

> When Jesus had finished telling these stories, he left and went to his hometown. He taught in their meeting place, and the people were so amazed that they asked, "Where does he get all this wisdom and the power to work these miracles? Isn't he the son of the carpenter? Isn't Mary his mother, and aren't James, Joseph, Simon, and Judas his brothers? Don't his sisters still live here in our town? How can he do all this?" So the people were very unhappy because of what he was doing. But Jesus said, "Prophets are honored by everyone, except the people of their hometown and their own family." And because the people did not have any faith, Jesus did not work many miracles there.
>
> —MATTHEW 13:53–58, CEV

Unbelief and familiarity are the death rattle to faith and the working of miracles. This is exactly what Jesus faced when He ministered in the Nazareth synagogue. Because of the attitude of His hometown residents, He did not do very many miracles there, which means that many in that very meeting place continued to deal with life-controlling problems, never accessing the supernatural ability of Jesus to deal with their issues once and for all. They were literally in the same room with the answer more times than they could count and went home as they had entered!

How could this happen? It happens every day! Believers continue carrying issues that God is able to deal with. What causes us to do such a thing? Unbelief and familiarity seem to be the culprits of our continuing condition. Most of us have decided that Jesus is Savior, but we are not sure He is healer. He is a friend, but is He really a miracle worker? He has healed others; will He really heal me?

No one in Nazareth doubted that there was something different about Jesus, but they had watched Him grow up and could not wrap their heads around Him being the Messiah. They knew His family and doubted that the promise of God could come from this family line.

This is probably the image in the mind of the woman with the spirit of infirmity on the day Jesus was teaching in the synagogue. Likely she had heard Him teach on several other occasions. He was certainly knowledgeable and anointed, but could all the reports of His miracles actually be true? If they were true, could He heal her? Would He heal her? Even if He could do such things, would she be worthy of such a miracle?

Whatever her thoughts, she never asked for the miracle. Look at how this went down. "When Jesus saw her, He called her to Him and said to her, 'Woman, you are loosed from your infirmity.' And

He laid His hands on her, and immediately she was made straight, and glorified God" (Luke 13:12–13).

Wow! What a great miracle, right? As we will learn later, not everyone was as excited as the woman who had been healed.

This story in Luke 13 bears a striking resemblance to the story of Michelle Hanson. Michelle and her husband, Dave, are pillars of the church. They attend services faithfully. They tithe financially and give liberally of their talents. Both are musicians who have served on their church's worship team over the years. They have taught Sunday school, led a youth scouting program, and home-schooled their five children.

Michelle and Dave are the kind of church members every pastor values highly. They are the kind of people that church leaders can call on, delegate to, and know the assignment will be taken care of with a spirit of excellence. God has anointed them to lead young people to Christ, and their steady, unselfish, dependable service has been an encouragement to their pastors and an inspiration to others in the congregation.

One might think that God's favor would protect these amazing individuals from life's tests and storms. Yet none are exempt from the trials of life! The thing is, "He makes His sun rise on the wicked and on the good, and makes the rain fall upon the upright and the wrongdoers [alike]" (Matt. 5:45, AMP). But as you will read in Michelle's story below, it was a lifelong trial that brought God nearer than she had ever known Him. She found Him "willing and able" when every other source and provision had been exhausted.

Are you in a similar situation? If you are, Michelle's words are sure to bring encouragement to you.

૭

A Normal Part of Life

I was born with spondylolisthesis, a condition of the spine caused when one vertebra slips forward or backward on to the next vertebra, causing extreme pain and often deformity. In my case, my lower lumbar vertebra slipped forward onto the sacrum. Besides this, my spinal column was twisted and contained an area that had no bone at all; it was only highly calcified.

Growing up, I often experienced pain in my back, but my parents said it was "growing pains" that would disappear when I reached adulthood. I believed everyone had pain like mine, that it was a normal part of life.

So, with grim determination, I managed to stay active through high school, even earning a spot as a jumper on the varsity track team. When the pain became strong enough to interfere with my focus, I took over-the-counter medicines such as Tylenol and aspirin. I also used a heating pad, ice, and Bengay to relax the muscles around my spine. A favorite thing was to apply Icy Hot then take a shower. That got the warmth down into my back. Because pain was part of my earliest memories, I believe I had developed a high tolerance for it.

My condition was not diagnosed until I was twenty-four years old. After giving birth to our second child, I was involved in an accident that required X-rays of my legs and pelvis. The orthopedic surgeon noticed something unusual. Concerned, he ordered spinal X-rays then diagnosed my birth defect.

As he explained spondylolisthesis, he told me it was the reason I was always in pain. He also told me that I was lucky. Giving birth could have caused a piece of the calcified area to break and double back on itself, severing my spinal column in the process. He went on to say that getting hit the wrong way or landing the wrong way in track could have done the same thing.

I realized at that point that God had been protecting me all my life. I can't remember how many times I had climbed trees, fences, and roofs to jump off them. As a child I thought that at the proper height and with the right umbrella I could fly like Mary Poppins. Hundreds of times I had practiced the high jump or long jump; on any of those occasions an unfortunate landing could have severed my spinal cord and left me paralyzed.

What I did not know my heavenly Father knew. He was true to His promise to be with me and keep me safe.

I didn't know what to make of the doctor's news. At first I questioned the Lord. "Why me? Why not my brother or someone else?" I never got answers, of course, but I did know that God made me the way I was for a reason; it was His choice.

My girls were four months old and two years old when the accident occurred; I was shocked to think that I could have been paralyzed just giving birth to them.

As the news sank in, I realized that having more children was simply not possible. I quickly asked the doctor about that. He told me we could have more, but the way I delivered them would have to change. I talked to the Lord about this. He assured me I could have the additional children I longed for, and these babies would be born safely and normally. I held on to that promise.

Certainly I prayed to be healed. As I did, the Holy Spirit told me something I couldn't put out of my mind. He said I would be healed, but "in My timing." As the years passed, I suffered through days when I thought death would have been better than living, but I never forgot those words. I knew that if I had to suffer, God knew about it and had a purpose for it.

He asked me a very interesting question at that time. "Is it enough to just ask Me?"

"Yes, Lord," I said. "You are the only one who can heal me."

After that I never asked anyone to pray for me. I prayed often that God would heal me, and others who knew of my pain would ask Him to deliver me from it, but I knew I could never ask anyone to pray for me. I would be healed "in His timing."

I took hold of Romans 8:28: "All things work together for good to those who love God, to those who are the called according to His purpose." During every Communion service I quoted the scripture that says, "By whose stripes you were healed" (1 Pet. 2:24), and applied those words to myself.

As a young wife and mother with a two-year-old and a four-month-old, I decided surgery would have to wait. And because I was nursing my daughter, I could not take narcotics, so I began using over-the-counter medications to take the edge off the pain. I also started seeing a chiropractic and massage therapist to help ease the hurting.

I can't say I changed the way I raised our children. I walked places with them, made crafts, and read with them. I stopped and bent over to talk with every animal they saw. But I did give up horseback riding and jogging; these were unnecessary risks. I stayed as active as possible with my kids because I did not want them to think their mom was different from other moms. I drove myself to participate in all their scouting activities, including camping and selling cookies, even while I wore a back brace.

One day I took the girls to dance practice, and another mom asked them how I was feeling.

"She's fine," they said. "Why are you asking?"

"Because you can see on her face that she's in pain," the friend answered.

"No, she's not," the girls said. "She hasn't said anything about pain."

I was glad to get that report. It meant I was successfully hiding the way I felt and not letting it interfere in their lives.

Over the next five years God gave me two more children. With age and the physical demands of family life, I advanced to Motrin to manage the pain. Most people take a couple of Motrin a day to relieve pain; I started with eight tablets and advanced to sixteen. The pain never went away. Pills did little more than make the pain tolerable so I could function.

My husband, David, was very supportive of me. He took on many duties that most husbands try to avoid. He helped with our homeschooling classes, and on days when I was hurting really bad, he worked from home to help with the children.

Then the day came when I decided I needed the surgery. I could put it off no longer.

The surgeon said he would graft bone taken from my hip and rib cages into my spinal column. Doing this would fuse my lower vertebrate together. I was warned I might lose movement in these vertebrate.

"Did I ever have movement in those areas?" I asked.

"No," the doctor replied.

"Well, then, I can't miss what I've never had, can I?"

After the surgery I spent five months in a back brace and began taking narcotics to control the pain. The doctor discovered that I had a negative reaction to morphine, but Demerol helped a lot. As time went on I added Darvocet, a powerful and addictive pain blocker available only by a doctor's prescription. At first I took 400 milligrams of Darvocet every two to three hours. The doctor was never concerned about how much I took; he prescribed more anytime I needed relief.

But the pain never went away. There was never a moment when my mind was not steeled to cope with agonizing pain. These strong medications did nothing more than put me to sleep, so I took them only if I was alone or my husband was home to watch the children.

Eventually I talked the doctor down to a lower dosage so I could control the drowsiness when I was home with four children. When Darvocet was pulled from the market, I switched to Vicodin.

Painkillers do more than kill pain. They can wipe you out. I began to understand drug addicts who take drugs so they can sleep for hours. When you sleep, there is no pain, and it doesn't matter if you are alone. It is coming back to reality that is painful.

As a child I did not realize that most people have no chronic pain, but as an adult I knew I was different. I wanted to be like everyone else. I also realized that my children needed a mother and my husband needed a wife, so I tried to hold out until bedtime each night before I took Darvocet or Vicodin. I knew being doped up was not healthy for my family. It was enough to suffer my own pain; I didn't want to bring pain to those I loved.

When I started physical therapy, the therapist told me the goal was to work on my back until all the pain moved into one spot. Then, she said, she would work the pain out of the one spot. I slipped away from my family long enough to attend physical therapy sessions three times a week.

Even so, I felt no change. I faithfully followed a regimen of exercises at home on the days I wasn't in a physical therapy session. No change. By 2012 I had been doing physical therapy daily for twelve years with no relief from my persistent, chronic pain.

Somehow the years passed and I survived. Relying on drugs to take the edge off the pain and help me function, I went about the strenuous job of homeschooling our children. I never missed a field trip with the kids; we went to one every other week for several years. The children participated in the annual science and history fairs.

I took on the role of soccer coach, assistant scout leader, and cookie mom. I made costumes for dance recitals and Christmas programs. I taught programs for teenage girls and young adults at the church. With God's help and strength I did my absolute best to support four wonderful children and an awesome husband. No one knew what I was going through in those days; it was enough to tell my heavenly Father alone.

In time pain wasn't the only issue I had to contend with. My spine itself was deteriorating. In the fall of 2010 I had surgery to regrow the cartilage in my knee. After surgery I was told not to lift any weight at all for eight weeks. Lying around was great for my knee but terrible for my back. By the time I learned to walk again, the pain in my back was severe most of the time.

I went back to my orthopedic surgeon and told him about the increased pain. An MRI showed cracks in my spinal column just above the bone grafts and cages. My doctor said the only way to fix the cracks was through more surgery. I asked him about the possibility of cracks above the new graft site. He said that, yes, in time new cracks would form. When they did, I would need even more cages and grafts, which would also develop cracks in time.

In other words, the problem would keep moving up my spinal column until my entire spinal column was grafted. Realizing I faced a crippling future dominated by debilitating pain, I turned down surgery.

The doctor suggested a series of spinal column injections of cortisone, which might help. I took three injections with no improvement. In fact, the only thing cortisone shots accomplished was to destroy my immune system and make my hair fall out! I ended up with reverse isolation until my immune system returned.

Apparently losing my immune system was a very rare side effect of the injections—so rare that no one bothered to tell me this could happen! It was at this point that my orthopedic surgeon let me know he could do no more, and I should come back when I was ready for additional surgery. He sent me away with prescriptions for powerful pain medications and muscle relaxers.

This was my life. I took medications to take the edge off the pain, and I continued my daily physical therapy. Pain was an intimate acquaintance.

By the fall of 2012 my pain was off the charts. I can't describe the intensity. Complicating the situation were muscle spasms that increased the pain. I was out of options and low on hope for any change. I conceded to the doctor's recommendation and decided I would need to have more surgery. I have gone through natural childbirth four times; the pain of childbirth was nothing compared to the pain I was having in my back.

By September 17 the muscles spasms were beyond bearable, and so was the pain. It was excruciating even for a woman who had borne it her entire life. These spasms and pain would not respond to medications or physical therapy, so I knew I would have to see my orthopedic surgeon soon.

That's where my condition had taken me on Sunday, September 23, 2012. That morning I went to church early to practice with the worship team before the service began. I was overwhelmed in practice by pain and spasms. I took medications and tried stretching, but I was not sure I could make it through the worship service.

The worship team always prays as practice ends and before the service begins. As we gathered by the altars to hold hands and ask for God to minister through us, several worship team members gathered around to pray for me. It was then the Lord spoke!

"You didn't ask. This is what you have been waiting for." He reminded me that I had obeyed by not asking others to pray for me; now, He was answering the desire of my heart.

The warmth of the Holy Spirit started to fill me. The team stopped praying, but I was still in pain. A woman praying before service noticed what was happening and asked, "Michelle, do you feel anything?" I told her what I was feeling, and she told the group, "Let's keep praying."

Time was not important; the start of morning service was lost from our minds. My team of worshippers continued praying, and this time as they prayed, I felt all the pain in my back merge into one single spot! Then I heard the Lord say, "It is finished."

At that exact moment the spot of pain disappeared! It was exactly what the physical therapist had described twelve years earlier but had not been able to do. The pain up and down my spine seemed to move into one small area, then disappear altogether in a moment! It happened "in His timing"! He was good to His word; I had only to wait for Him!

I sang my praises with a loud voice that wonderful morning! I went home and tested myself, flexing and turning and bending to see if my miracle was really a hoax. No pain! No hoax! I was really, really healed!

A few weekends later I took my place on the church's kick ball team and scored three runs! I ran the bases like I had in high school. I don't plan to run a marathon, but I enjoyed running those bases.

My doctor said I could call him anytime I need to renew a drug prescription. I haven't called him in a good long time.

Looking back I can see God's hand through all this. I never severed my spinal column. I never became addicted to pain medications. When I had given up and acquiesced for more surgery, the Lord "in His timing" came near and healed me. I am now pain-free for the first time in my entire life!

∾

JESUS FOUND HER

The lady in Luke 13 did not approach Jesus for her miracle; He called her out and literally straightened her spine. For years Michelle did not ask anyone to pray for her healing; she just waited until someone came to her. In essence, on September 23, 2012, Jesus called to Michelle through a group of musicians and praise team members and straightened and strengthened her spine.

Not everyone was happy with the miracle Jesus performed in the synagogue that day in Nazareth. One would think the healing of a woman being bowed over, unable to stand up straight, for eighteen years would bring great joy to everyone who knew her. But in reality her miracle initiated a heated dialogue about whether it was legal to heal on the Sabbath day.

Jesus did not back down. He took on the ruler of the synagogue, and when He was finished, the entire group was praising and glorifying God.

There are many in our day who do not believe in miracles and speak despairingly of those who do. The truth is, God is still in the miracle business and desires to do for each of us what He did for the woman in Luke 13 and Michelle Hanson.

Can you believe the Lord for your miracle right now? Pray this prayer with me:

> *Dear Lord Jesus, I am tired of living like this. I have carried this problem as far as I can. I am now ready to lay it at Your feet. I know it is not Your will for me to go through life bowed over with this infirmity. I give it to*

You right now and expect Your miracle-working power to touch and completely heal me. Just as You healed Michelle and the lady in Luke 13, I receive this miracle from You now. I praise You for this miracle. It is mine, and I receive it in the name that is above every name, the name of Jesus. Amen.

Sixteen

IS GRACE ENOUGH?

THE STORIES OF modern-day miracles cannot help but encourage us to believe God for the things that threaten our lives and happiness. Nothing can take the place of the audacity of a sincere person believing God and praying a hole through the sky. Yet there is a time to pray and a time to act. Once we have prayed and believe God has heard our prayer, we must act in faith, knowing the grace of God is at work in our lives. When it comes to the grace of God, we can:

- Sing about it and never understand it
- Discuss it and never exhaust it
- Debate it and never fully comprehend it
- Receive it and never completely grasp it
- Display it and never really have a handle on it
- Ignore it and never outrun it

The greatest gift available to mankind is the grace of God. Jesus came to bring about a new dispensation of time. It is interesting to note that the dispensation He introduced would become known as the dispensation of grace! He lived thirty-three years, but until He left earth for heaven, grace was no more than a rumor.

Until Christ finished His work on the cross, grace was only a figment of man's wildest imagination. Now Jesus has returned to heaven, and grace has become a reality for all humankind.

If Jesus left grace for us, how do we receive it? "For by grace you have been saved through faith, and that not of yourselves; *it is the gift of God*, not of works, lest anyone should boast" (Eph. 2:8–9, emphasis added). We receive grace by accepting it as a gift!

The word *grace* is mentioned one hundred seventy times in the King James Version of the Bible. It is a very, very important subject!

What is the difference between grace and mercy? Most of us merge the two meanings together when, in fact, they are enormously different. Mercy is *not getting what I deserve*; grace is *getting what I do not deserve!*

Not one person whose story has been told in these pages deserved a miracle. None of us do. Rather than earning a miracle on their own merits, grace delivered a knockout punch to their problems and secured a miracle on their behalf. No matter what you are facing, the grace of God is capable of doing the same for you. All we must do is pray, believe, and receive.

The theologians of old often talked about *prevenient* grace. The word *prevenient* comes from the word *prevent*, which, as it appears in the English Bible, is often misunderstood. Usually we think the word *prevent* means to stop or hinder something. If I say I prevented someone from driving a car, it could be thought that I kept that person from doing so. But the meaning of the word *prevent* today is far different from its meaning when the King James Version was first translated. The word appears twice in the King James Version of the New Testament, and neither means "to stop" or "to hinder."

The first instance is in Matthew 17:24–27: "And when they were come to Capernaum, they that received tribute money came to Peter, and said, Doth not your master pay tribute? He saith, Yes.

And when he was come into the house, Jesus *prevented* him, saying, What thinkest thou, Simon? of whom do the kings of the earth take custom or tribute? of their own children, or of strangers? Peter saith unto him, Of strangers. Jesus saith unto him, Then are the children free. Notwithstanding, lest we should offend them, go thou to the sea, and cast an hook, and take up the fish that first cometh up; and when thou hast opened his mouth, thou shalt find a piece of money: that take, and give unto them for me and thee" (KJV, emphasis added).

The Greek word used in this verse is *prophthanō*, and it means "to anticipate."[1] Jesus did not prevent or stop Peter from doing something; instead, He anticipated Peter's thoughts and actions.

The second use of the word *prevent* is in 1 Thessalonians 4:14–15: "If we believe that Jesus died and rose again, even so them also which sleep in Jesus will God bring with him. For this we say unto you by the word of the Lord, that we which are alive and remain unto the coming of the Lord shall not *prevent* them which are asleep" (KJV, emphasis added).

Here the Greek word is *phthanō*, and means "to come before, precede."[2] The word *prevent* in this verse does not mean that those who are alive at the coming of the Lord will stop those who have already passed on, only that we will not precede them in the Rapture.

In both instances where the word *prevent* is used in the New Testament, it means to anticipate or to precede. Prevenient grace, then, is that grace that goes before and is, in effect, independent of human involvement. Every believer can look back and see this prevenient grace at work in his or her life. Dr. A. H. Strong says, "The old theologians talked of 'prevenient grace'—grace that lays hold of us before we know it, and prepares us for the emergencies of the future."[3]

GRACE THAT GETS THERE FIRST

Prevenient grace is grace that gets there first. When we begin to realize that His grace arrives on the scene before we know danger exists, we will feel better about all our tomorrows. Think of this:

1. **Grace already existed before man sinned in the garden.** As soon as the sin of Adam and Eve was exposed, God walked into the garden and announced the punishment of the serpent and rolled out a plan for man's redemption. The plan of salvation was never plan B; it was always plan A! How do we know that? Jesus was "the Lamb slain from the foundation of the world" (Rev. 13:8, KJV). This scripture makes clear that the sacrifice for sin had been decided before Adam and Eve ever sinned. Grace got there first!

2. **Grace furnished the strength for Noah as he built and boarded the ark.** Through grace God gave him the strength and perseverance to complete the project that would sustain human life. Before Noah started working, God sent grace.

3. **Grace sustained Elijah despite death threats and drought.** Before Elijah ever arrived at the brook Cherith, God provided ravens to airlift food to him and caused the stream to continue running despite the drought (1 Kings 17:1–6). Grace got there first.

4. **Grace never ceased despite Samson's sin.** Grace is not dispensed based on our personal merits. It is offered freely. Samson turned his heart back to God

and was surprised to discover that grace was there all along.

5. **Grace propelled the first-century believers even though the path was difficult.** Despite extreme persecution the first-century church discovered that grace was present in houses, courtrooms, jail cells, and the public square. Grace got there before persecution began.

In our culture we are conditioned to believe "you get what you pay for." Yet:

- Grace cannot be earned. One cannot work hard enough to earn the grace of God.

- One cannot be good enough to deserve it. Grace is getting what I do not deserve.

- One cannot be acquainted with enough people to leverage it. Grace is not dispensed based on how many powerful people one knows; grace is given freely.

In Matthew's account of the dialogue between Jesus and Peter, grace was present *before* the taxes were due. When Peter broke the news to Jesus about the tax issue, Jesus did not say, "Let Me get back to you on that." He told Peter what to do to make the taxes current. Before the issue surfaced, a plan was already in place to resolve it. That's called grace!

Grace also was present *when* the taxes came due. Peter was upset to discover that Jesus owed a tax bill and he was being assessed as well. When Jesus revealed where the funds were to pay the taxes (in the mouth of a fish), He promised enough funds to settle both His and Peter's bills. That's what I call grace!

Grace was already present even though they did not owe the taxes. Jesus made it very clear that neither of them owed the taxes being charged them, but to maintain a stellar reputation, they paid. Jesus was telling Peter, "We do not owe what they are assessing, but don't worry about it; this is not going to cost either of us anything because My Father has made a deposit in the mouth of a fish that is enough to settle the entire account." This is grace that got there first.

Grace made a way where there seemed to be no way! Isn't that the way grace always works? That's why it has been lovingly called amazing!

Can we count on grace to be there when we need it most? *Yes!*

Grace reigned in eternity past. Jesus was slain "from the foundation of the world" (Rev. 13:8, kjv). Search the Old Testament, and you will discover that even though the people were living under law, grace could be seen everywhere. God cannot help Himself! He furnishes grace in all situations. According to Revelation 13 and 1 Peter 1, a covenant of grace existed in eternity past, evidence of grace that got here first. If God made provision for the redemption of man before there ever was a man, then He has already taken care of tomorrow's problems today. Grace is not what God does; it is who He is.

Grace reigns in real time. Jesus was "foreordained before the foundation of the world, but was manifest in these last times" (1 Pet. 1:20, kjv). In real time He is administrating or executing grace as He planned long ago!

A chief financial officer has the responsibility of administering the finances of a company. One of the primary responsibilities of a CFO is to make certain all financial obligations are paid in a timely fashion. When a check is sent out to meet a financial obligation of that company, at some point it has passed through the hands of the CFO. Jesus is the administrator of grace. When you receive grace, dust it for fingerprints, and you will discover it has passed through God's loving hands on its way to you. Grace reigns in real time, as in *right now*! Get ready for grace!

Grace will reign in eternity to come. Grace has always been and will always be. Grace is getting what we do not deserve. We have experienced grace our entire lives, and we are promised heaven in the world to come. That is what I call grace!

The grace of God covers us when we least deserve it. The difficulty many have in believing God will furnish grace to get us through our crisis is that we do not believe we deserve it. Again, grace is simply getting what I do not deserve.

The grace of God shows up with is the key to release us from our fiercest bondages. All of us have been delivered from something, and the truth is, all of us probably still need a deliverance or two in our lives. The good news is that He is a delivering God. The apostle Paul said God has "delivered us from so great a death, and doth deliver: in whom we trust that he will yet deliver us" (2 Cor. 1:10, KJV). This scripture places grace in our past, present, and future.

Grace intervenes when sin is present. When we have allowed ourselves to become involved in sinful practices, grace is constantly knocking on the door of our hearts. Can you hear what the Spirit is saying when sin is present? "Listen! I am standing and knocking at your door. If you hear my voice and open the door, I will come in and we will eat together" (Rev 3:20, CEV). The truth is, grace makes horrible sinners of us. While we are sinning, grace is constantly knocking on the door of the heart, attempting to deliver what we do not deserve.

Grace opens doors that were shut permanently to us. Everyone has experienced situations where a door was shut and there appeared no way to open it. Then as quickly as it was shut, the door opened again. That is what grace looks like.

Grace provides a way of escaping judgment. Everyone deserves to be judged for his or her mistakes and failures, but grace vacates the sentence and bestows blessing. Grace changed our eternal destiny from hell to heaven. That's what grace does!

Peter discovered that grace arrives before the crisis develops. Before the taxes were due, the grace of God was present. Every person whose story is on display in this book discovered this to be true as well. As each of them looked back over their crisis, they realized God had furnished His grace before they knew it would be needed.

Jesus declared, "Your Father knows the things you have need of before you ask Him" (Matt. 6:8). This is the ultimate prevenient grace. Before we ask, He is at work. With each challenge we face, we can count on grace to get there first. We do not know what tomorrow holds, but we know who holds tomorrow. The hand that holds our future is full of grace and truth.

Peter, as well as each person mentioned in this book, discovered that grace remained as long as the crisis persisted. It is difficult for us to know just how long our dilemma is going to last, but we know the grace of God will outlast it. When we are walking through a tough time, a few days or weeks can feel like an eternity, but we can rest assured that grace will be present for as long as our problem lingers.

Peter and every person mentioned in these stories came to understand that grace will remain until the exit strategy has been carried out. In each of our crisis situations in life, grace holds the door for our exit and does not leave the scene until we are a safe distance away. Looking back over my life, I can testify to this occurring again and again.

Will there be enough grace for each challenge we face? Yes! Listen to the words of Paul in 2 Corinthians 12:7–9: "Lest I should be exalted above measure by the abundance of the revelations, a thorn in the flesh was given to me, a messenger of Satan to buffet me, lest I be exalted above measure. Concerning this thing I pleaded with the Lord three times that it might depart from me. And He said to me, 'My grace is sufficient for you, for My strength is made perfect in weakness.'"

Over the years I have heard numerous people talking about Paul's "thorn in the flesh." Some say it was sickness or a myriad of other things, but the scripture clearly says it was a "messenger of Satan" sent to cause him trouble.

Literally everywhere Paul went, he had a revival and caused a riot, in that order. These problems were the result of a message that went counter to the religious establishment of his day. The message he preached was a threat to the livelihood of religious bureaucrats. Add to this the fact that he had been one of them and then changed his allegiance to the upstart church at Jerusalem. He began to proclaim that Jesus was in fact the Messiah and the religious establishment had killed Him. Because of this, they came after him with a vengeance.

Though Paul experienced staunch opposition everywhere he went and his opponents would not let up, God assured him His grace would be more than enough. The reason God would not be delivering Paul from the opposition was because the propagation of the Word of God was more important than Paul's comfort. The fact that God was not going to deliver him did not mean that God was going to leave him to fend for himself. Quite the contrary is true; God was going to:

- Make a deposit of grace before Paul arrived in each place

- Assign grace to remain as long as Paul was present

- Make sure the grace Paul received would be more than enough

- Guarantee that grace would linger long after Paul's departure

No matter what we go through, we must remember, grace belongs to us! It is here for us! The only question remaining is whether we will accept it or reject it.

Scripture tells us it is possible to frustrate the grace of God. "I do not frustrate the grace of God: for if righteousness come by the law, then Christ is dead in vain" (Gal. 2:21, KJV). If grace is a gift from God, how could one frustrate this gift? The grace of God is frustrated if we:

- Add to it

- Restrict it

- Take away from it

- Delineate from its power

- Relegate it to an inferior position

When one needs a miracle, grace will be the delivery truck it arrives in. Grace is getting what I do not deserve. For various reasons we often find it difficult to accept the miracle grace is attempting to deliver, and in so doing, we frustrate the grace of God. When we frustrate the grace of God, we fail to sign the delivery receipt for our miracle.

While audacious prayer is necessary, we must reach a point where we believe *God wants us to have what we are praying for* and be expectantly awaiting the delivery truck of grace. C. H. Spurgeon said, "The Lord will go through with His covenant engagements. Whatever He takes in hand He will accomplish; hence past mercies are guarantees for the future and admirable reasons for continuing to cry unto Him."[4]

I think I hear the beep-beep-beep of the delivery truck of grace backing up to your life right now! Go quickly and sign the delivery receipt to your miracle!

NOTES

CHAPTER ONE

1. Cameron V. Thompson, *Master Secrets of Prayer* (Madison, GA: Light for Living Publications, 1990).
2. Peter J. Kreeft, *Angels and Demons: What Do We Really Know About Them?* (San Francisco: Ignatius Press, 1995), 23.
3. Thomas Watson, *A Body of Practical Divinity* (Cheapside, London: n.p., 1692).
4. Matthew Henry and Thomas Scott, A *Commentary Upon the Holy Bible: Genesis to Deuteronomy* (London: The Religious Tract Society, 1836), 156.
5. ThinkExist.com, "Winston Churchill Quotes," http://thinkexist.com/quotation/the_nose_of_the_bulldog_has_been_slanted/177150.html (accessed September 23, 2013).

CHAPTER THREE

1. Blue Letter Bible, "Dictionary and Word Search for *aggareuō* (Strong's 29)," http://www.blueletterbible.org/lang/lexicon/lexicon .cfm?Strongs=G29&t=KJV (accessed September 23, 2012).

CHAPTER SIXTEEN

1. Blue Letter Bible, "Dictionary and Word Search for *prophthanō* (Strong's 4399)," http://www.blueletterbible.org/lang/lexicon/lexicon .cfm?Strongs=G4399&t=KJV (accessed September 26, 2013).
2. Blue Letter Bible, "Dictionary and Word Search for *phthanō* (Strong's 5348)," http://www.blueletterbible.org/lang/lexicon/lexicon .cfm?Strongs=G5348&t=KJV (accessed September 26, 2013).
3. Augustus Hopkins Strong, *One Hundred Chapel-Talks to Theological Students* (Philadelphia: The Griffith & Rowland Press, 1913), 148. Viewed at Google Books.
4. As quoted in L. B. Cowman, *Streams in the Desert* (Grand Rapids, MI: Zondervan, 1996), 160. Viewed at Google Books.

EMPOWERED
TO RADICALLY CHANGE
YOUR WORLD

FREE NEWSLETTERS
TO HELP EMPOWER YOUR LIFE

Why subscribe today?

❑ **DELIVERED DIRECTLY TO YOU.** All you have to do is open your inbox and read.

❑ **EXCLUSIVE CONTENT.** We cover the news overlooked by the mainstream press.

❑ **STAY CURRENT.** Find the latest court rulings, revivals, and cultural trends.

❑ **UPDATE OTHERS.** Easy to forward to friends and family with the click of your mouse.

CHOOSE THE E-NEWSLETTER THAT INTERESTS YOU MOST:

- Christian news
- Daily devotionals
- Spiritual empowerment
- And much, much more

SIGN UP AT: **http://freenewsletters.charismamag.com**

8178